DIRECT MAIL MASTERY

Direct Mail Insight That Will Increase Your Expertise and Make You Money!

By T.J. Rohleder

America's Blue Jeans Millionaire

Other Titles by T.J. Rohleder:

The Blue Jeans Millionaire
How to Turn Your Kitchen or Spare Bedroom into a Cash Machine
The Black Book of Marketing Secrets (Series)
The Ruthless Marketing Attack
How to Get Super Rich in the Opportunity Market
Five Secrets That Will Triple Your Profits
Ruthless Copywriting Strategies
Ruthless Marketing
50 in 50
Secrets of the Blue Jeans Millionaire
How to Make Millions Sitting on Your Ass

For information address:

M.O.R.E. Incorporated • 305 E. Main St. • Goessel, KS 67053-0198

FIRST EDITION
ISBN 1-933356-78-2

TABLE OF CONTENTS

<u>INTRODUCTION</u>

Hello, and welcome to *Direct Mail Mastery*! Expect this to be an exciting book—one that can change your life and improve your entire business, assuming you'll actually put the tips I teach you here into direct action.

Now, I know that may sound like hype, precisely the sort of thing you'd expect to hear from a motivational publication. Sorry; this isn't one of those books. This is a book about making more sales and profits to your existing customers *and* to the new customers you can attract through direct mail. It's purely factual, not hype at all. As surely as spring follows winter, if you constructively use the tips, tricks and strategies I'll outline here, then you really *will* change your life and business. This will give you a genuine, unfair advantage over your competitors—the kind of advantage that can help you succeed to the tune of millions of dollars.

You see, most of your competition doesn't know anything about direct mail marketing. At best, they think it's just mailing postcards or flyers. They have no clue as to how to go about making money with direct mail marketing, which we like to call "stealth marketing." Think of those stealth fighter jets designed to fool enemy radar, and you've got the idea. Good direct mail marketing sneaks by underneath the competitor's radar. Done correctly, they'll have no idea you're doing it at all.

Direct mail helps you convince more of the very best prospective buyers in your marketplace to do business with you instead of the competition. You can dramatically increase your sales and profits, build your business, and they won't have a clue why. No other marketing method we know of gives you that advantage. So in these pages, I'll share the tips, tricks, and strategies that have generated millions of dollars for me, my clients, my colleagues, and many other small business people and entrepreneurs who have learned how to master the secrets of direct mail marketing.

My name is T.J. Rohleder, and I'm cofounder of M.O.R.E., Inc of Goessel, Kansas. I first discovered the secrets of direct mail marketing from a man I consider a mentor: Russ von Hoelscher. My wife Eileen and I met Russ in the spring of 1989. At that time, we'd been in the business for about six months, running small ads in national magazines to sell a unique product we'd developed. Russ saw several of our ads and sent us a brochure for his consulting services. He included a friendly little note that said, "I like what you're doing. I think I can help you make more money. Give me a call."

When I picked up that phone and dialed his number, our business was transformed. We went from making $16,000 a month (based on an initial investment of just $300, by the way) to making $400,000 a month within nine months. In our first five years of business, we generated a grand total of over $10 million in gross sales, mostly because Russ taught us the secrets of making money with direct mail. What Russ has done for me, I'd like to do for you. Not only does it profit me by telling you in this venue, I appreciate the competition—and there's plenty of room here at the top.

If you run a business and you're not using direct mail

marketing, you're making a terrible mistake. Most of your competition doesn't even understand direct mail, so you can absolutely dynamite them when you start it. They won't even know what hit them.

Direct mail has been very, very good to me, and the same can be said of Russ von Hoelscher and some of his other clients. Personally, my company has made over $150,000,000 with it. Not everyone has done that well with it, but he does have other clients who have become multi-millionaires.

Let me reiterate: direct mail is superb as a sales medium, *once you learn how to do it right.* Some people tell me they tried direct mail once and got little or no results, so they gave up on it. That's because they did it wrong. If that's your story, I guarantee you're on the right track now. This book will have you aggressively, successfully squeezing profit from an infinite source of money. When you know how to do it properly, and leverage good products and services, your profits will skyrocket.

Not to be cocky, but I believe that my enthusiasm for this book's subject matter, not just the subject matter itself, will help you adapt more easily to direct mail. I can bring a lot of positive energy and optimism to the table, because I know how well it works—and I love teaching it to other people. Even if you feel you've failed before, I know I can teach you to make it work—if you're serious, and willing to follow just a few logical rules. Again, it can be ultra-successful when done correctly. That's not to say that every promotion or campaign you do will be a success, but when you have the core ingredients in place and do things the right way, you set yourself up for success.

I'll be discussing a number of strategies in these chapters that I feel you need to know in order to have the greatest opportunity for success. While direct mail can work wonders when done right, there are many ways to do it wrong...and that's why some people are less than enthusiastic about it. Their methods are or were unsuccessful, souring them on the whole field. This book will set you on the right path. I'll help you figure out how to do things properly, by showing you what worked for us and others—including some of the great masters of direct response marketing (DRM), and strategies they've taught for many years. This is a tried-and-true method of producing results for your business.

One of the best things about direct mail is that it's accountable for results in a way most marketing isn't. With traditional "shotgun" marketing, you often have no clue whether your ads are working or not. Was it the print ad that brought people in, word of mouth, a billboard, or a TV spot? Who knows? If you did know, you could focus your marketing dollars there. Direct mail lets you do that. Just hoping something makes money, as most ad companies do, is a scary way to handle your advertising.

With direct mail, you know exactly how much you've spent running an ad or sending out sales letters, brochures, and flyers for your business. Then you know how much business has come in as a result, and from whom. That's one of the best reasons why direct mail is useful for your business—it helps you nail down those costs and figure out exactly where you're spending money effectively, and where you're wasting it.

One of the things you'll quickly learn as an entrepreneur or business owner is that you'll never learn it all—and that's certainly true of direct mail. There are always new methodologies and variables to explore, new things to learn. School is never out for the pro. So even if you've been at it a while, I think you'll benefit greatly from this book. At the very least, my intention is to stir in you a desire to learn more, and to help you discover the strategies that I and others have used for direct mail success.

Some of the things I'll discuss are specific, actionable strategies you can easily put into place, while some of my topics will be more conceptual. All are core strategies—and I think it's going to be an exciting ride for you. So get ready to take notes, write in the margins, underline passages, add a sticky tab here and there, and limber up your favorite highlighter. Grab your favorite beverage, sharpen your mind, and dive right in.

CHAPTER 1:
The Main Advantages
of Direct Mail

In the introduction, I pointed out that direct mail can change your entire life and business philosophy—and how that sounded like so much hype. But that's exactly happened to me and my wife. When Eileen and I met Russ von Hoelscher, we were doing no direct mail at all. We were running space ads in national magazines and using the proceeds to buy more ads—just as a lot of other small business people are still doing. We focused on chasing after new customers, which is a huge mistake. One of the things Russ taught us to do was to mine the money available in reselling to *existing* customers.

We used to hire Russ to come to our home in Kansas and work with us over the weekend. At that time, Russ charged us $2,500 for a weekend of his time and expertise. Nowadays, if you could even get him to that, it would cost you four or five times more, and would *still* be worth every dollar. I know I'm slightly biased, but Russ is a master when it comes to making money with direct mail. I was privileged to watch the master go to work. We'd pick him up at the airport on a Friday night and, starting very early Saturday morning, we'd sit around the dining room table and talk about all kinds of products and services our customers might be interested in, as well as new promotions. Then Russ would get excited about something that we were talking about, and he would start writing. We always had big stacks of legal pads waiting for him there.

Meanwhile, Eileen and I would sit back in awe, watching him writing fast and furious, as quickly as he could; and when he'd stop, we'd talk more, drink some more coffee, and eat some good food. Then he'd be at it again. He was taking all the ideas we were expressing, and clearly translating them onto his legal pads as he wrote the sales letters. When he left on Sunday, I'd stop by the typist's house and drop off all those pads to have them typed out and saved to a floppy disk. Then I'd tweak the copy he wrote, send the resulting sales letters out to our customers, and start raking in the profits.

Within a few weeks, checks, money orders, and even cash would came pouring in——and I got to see it all live, up close, and personal. Somewhere along the line while watching Russ do his work, I said to myself, "I want to learn how to do this." It took me a long time to learn it——and I'm still learning. It's a fascinating, lifelong process.

It *sounds* simple, but doing it well is not. Sure, it's just a matter of taking ideas for new, related products and services, writing simple sales letters communicating them, putting them into envelopes, and sending them to your best customers—— people who have already bought something from you before. That's as simple as it can be. But most businesses aren't doing that. They're doing what Eileen and I did before we met Russ. They're constantly chasing new customers; they're not doing enough to sell additional products to their existing customers.

That was our entry into direct mail. Once we started

using direct mail to sell to our existing customers, Russ helped us learn how to use direct mail to create sales letters for *new* customers—those who were interested in the kinds of things we were selling, but had never done business with us before. That's when the millions came pouring in.

You get an incredible feeling when you put together your first direct mail package and the orders start pouring in. It's exciting, addictive, and profitable—and I'll cover all that in depth in this book. So: let's take a look at the main advantages of direct mail marketing.

Advantage #1: Direct mail *works*. It's like a recipe: Follow the instructions, and you'll get the results you desire. Forget that so many other people aren't using it. Don't be restricted by the fact that may it not have worked for you before. You didn't know then what you'll know by the time you finish reading this book.

Advantage #2: It works for everyone, including small businesses. In your local marketplace, you probably won't have much direct mail competition, if any. You'll have a chance to run right past your competitors and become the dominant business in your field. Even if you run a regional or national business, the chances are good that none of your competitors are doing what you can do with direct mail.

Advantage #3: Direct mail is targeted marketing. You can pick and choose people who have bought services and products similar to yours in the past. Most other forms of advertising don't allow this. Those methods waste most of your advertising on people who aren't interested in what you offer.

The readers, listeners, and viewers are part of a big shotgun market of people from all walks of life, just a tiny fraction of whom are your best prospects. Direct mail makes it so easy for you to choose the people you want to reach—and then to reach them in a personal way. You're actually sending a letter to someone, communicating via a printed letter, one-on-one. Always act as though you have something special to say to one special person. That's what makes direct mail so personable.

Advantage #4. Almost no one knows these secrets. If they know anything about direct mail, it's typically very basic; they understand it involves mailing things to prospects, usually postcards. They may have tried it, and found it didn't work for them. Again, that's because they're doing it wrong. They don't understand the industry or the methods—not even the basics, let alone its intricacies. As shipping magnate Aristotle Onassis once said, "The secret to business is to know something nobody else knows." That's true of direct mail. If you can learn to understand direct mail marketing at a basic level, and you're willing to focus your efforts on it, the rest can come later. It takes a lifetime to master, but you can earn while you learn.

Advantage #5: Direct mail gives you an unbeatable lead, almost an unfair advantage, over other marketers. It's a stealthy way to promote your offers to your marketplace, because your competitors may have no idea what you're doing. The only way they'll learn is if someone tells them, or if they get on your mailing list somehow.

Advantage #6: Direct mail marketing is scalable, whether up or down. With an initial test, when you're just getting started with an offer, you'll want to keep the volume low. If the market responds, you crank the dial up, mailing out more pieces. If it doesn't, you try another offer. Whether or not you scale up and down may also depend on the marketplace you're in. If the whole Internet is your marketplace and you have millions of potential customers, then even a small return may make it worth cranking up the volume. If you're in a small local economy, with thousands or tens of thousands of potential customers at most, you'll require a greater response. Always check your numbers and always test, and you can continue to grow your business.

If you don't think you can handle all that work yourself, hire more employees. This is especially true if you're a one-man band, because your ability to grow is limited by your ability to perform. Let other people do some of the work; act as the brain behind it, the person who directs and facilitates it. This method can work whether you mow lawns for a living, own a small mechanic shop, or you're an electrician and think you don't need to advertise because you have all the business you can handle right now. Build a team you pay to do most of the actual work. Don't get stuck by thinking small.

Advantage #7: You can segment your customer list, so certain offers go out to specific groups of customers. Your very best customers—the people who spend the most money with you—will get offers the rest of your customers don't; so even within your customer base, there's stealth selling going on. Your other lists, won't even see an offer unless it's a hit with your best customers, whereupon you carefully introduce it to everyone you think might buy it.

Advantage #8: You can make grand offers with a much

better chance of success than most advertising methods. One of my personal heroes is P.T. Barnum, one the founders of the Ringling Brothers, Barnum and Bailey circus. He was an incredible entrepreneur, involved in all kinds of businesses. Many good biographies have been written on the man, and it's worth it to study his life—because he understood marketing at a deep level, which helped him become one of the world's richest men in his day.

I'll repeat a certain P.T. Barnum quote several times in this book, because it's an important one: "Most business people are trying to catch a whale using a minnow as bait." They throw together direct mail flyers, self-mailers, or postcards that aren't connected to any kind of strategy. Those campaigns fail to produce, so they give up and declare that direct mail doesn't work. Nothing could be further from the truth. One of the things I'll show you in this book is how to use the inexpensive methods correctly.

Many people are enamored by Internet or online marketing; I am too, but I don't accept it as the be-all and end-all of marketing. It's anything but. Direct mail beats the pants off *all* other kinds of marketing and advertising methods, but it especially beats anything people can do on the Internet, hands down. You'll see one of the reasons for that with our next advantage:

Advantage #9: Done correctly, direct mail marketing does a complete job of selling. It's like a salesperson in an envelope—one who never gets sick, never complains, never wants a raise, and works 24 hours a day. If done correctly, it's disruptive—which is precisely what you want it to be. I was involved in the business for years before I really understood the full impact of the word. Direct mail *has* to be disruptive in order to catch people's attention. Yes, people still sort their mail over a trash can sometimes, not paying close attention to all the direct mail they're getting; but it's still far more disruptive than any other method, except for a live salesperson.

Think about how easy it is to delete your e-mail; you don't even have to read it. Direct mail is far more disruptive than email; it gets in the way and drives in that little wedge that's necessary in order to get the right people to pay attention. It seems like everybody's in love with whatever's new, and direct mail is old-fashioned—so most people ignore it. Yes, it's old news, but it works better than all those fancy innovations.

Advantage #10: Direct mail can make you big money. My company has generated over $150 million in gross direct mail revenue in 24 years, and my wife and I are the most average people you'll ever meet; you'd never pick us out of a lineup of successful people. Yet, direct mail marketing has been responsible for almost all of the millions of dollars that have come pouring into our little company. Our headquarters are in Goessel, Kansas. If you didn't know it was an hour north of Wichita, you wouldn't be able to find it on a map. You probably still wouldn't find it.

Now, we love Kansas and are passionate about our state, but we also recognize it for what it is. It's pretty much in the middle of nowhere, and we like it that way. But although we're in a town of just a few hundred people, we're generating millions of dollars with direct mail. That should inspire you. This is something that really *can* make you a lot of money.

Before we move on to the next chapter, I want to add one more thing. If there's a single business tip that will profit you more than any other, it's this: you have to sell more things to more people more often for more profit with every transaction. Everything is details. But such details! You have to figure out all the ways and means, strategies and methods; and you have to get it all correct. But it's still just selling more to more people more often for more profit per transaction. Direct mail marketing is the ultimate way to do that. You're in full control of every aspect of the process.

Yes, there's a learning curve. You have to be willing to both learn and practice. In this book, I'll try to make it fun and exciting for you. But even if you don't feel that way about it—as I think you will—just keep your eyes on the prize. You can earn incredible amounts of money while you're learning, and even more when you've mastered direct mail. There's simply no better way to use that little formula of selling more stuff to more people more often for more profit every time than direct mail.

There's so much opportunity here, and plenty of room for you to excel. The two most important things with direct mail are the list you use and the words you say—the copywriting—so I'll also provide tips on copywriting in this book. Having written copy for years, I know it's not something you can learn to do well quickly. But you *can* learn to do it, if you're willing to put in the time and effort. Now, you don't have to do your own copywriting at all if you don't have the passion for it; there are professional copywriters who will gladly charge you money to do it for you. But if you go that route, be very careful—and always deal with a professional who understands direct mail. The local guys at the PennySaver or the Thrifty Nickel may want to do a little moonlighting for you, but in my experience they're not top copywriters.

Russ von Hoelscher offers a sort of unique "in-between" copywriting service that costs just a tiny fraction of what he'd charge to write it from scratch. If you write your own direct mail copy and send it to him, he'll tell you what's good about it and what you should throw out. If you're interested in that, call him at 619-588-2155.

That said, I still recommend that you focus on writing your own copy, even if you do run it past Russ. So don't just read this book once; read it multiple times, so you can learn the skill set necessary to make money with direct mail. Dig in deep and really use these methods I'll teach you here, and you'll be light years ahead of the competition.

CHAPTER 2:
Direct Mail Errors

Some people say direct mail doesn't work for small businesses—the mercantile backbone of this great nation. But they're wrong; it works very well for *all* businesses when handled correctly. If it doesn't work it's because it's being done wrong—period. In this chapter, I'll discuss nine top direct mail marketing mistakes and how to avoid them.

Here's an interesting case study about how direct mailing can go wrong. Several years ago, the owner of a carpet cleaning company in Columbus, Ohio decided to try direct mail for the first time. Let's call him Tom. He connected with a list company, rented a list of people with zip codes in his area, then mailed out a few thousand pieces offering a discount to new customers. Within a couple of weeks, he was convinced it bombed; he got *one* new customer. He decided direct-mail just didn't work.

And he was right: it didn't work the way he did it. The problem was, Tom's business was located in a low-rent neighborhood. There's nothing wrong with that; the problem was, Tom's entire zip code was nothing but low-rent neighborhoods, with a mix of low-end businesses and people who lived mostly in apartment buildings. Even 90% of those living in houses rented. Those are *not* the right kinds of customers for carpet cleaning, as I know from personal experience; my first business was a carpet cleaning business. To make a sad story a joyful one, Tom was finally convinced to do it the right way. He did a mailing to people in a neighborhood just two or three miles away, where most people owned their own homes—and business went through the roof.

This sort of direct mail misfire is common, and it's what sours so many people on it. They don't do a professional job, in that they fail to capture people's attention and interest and make them respond, or they just mail to the wrong people.

That's **Direct Mail Mistake #1:** Lack of focus. If you're going to rent a mailing list, you'd better do some research into the type of list you need to succeed. All Tom needed was residents who had nice properties and took good care of their homes. Keep that in mind, especially if you're selling something expensive: you have to go to the people who have the money. For other types of businesses, it's smart to go with a mailing list of people who have bought something similar to what you have for sale.

There is nothing more important to direct mail than the mailing list.

Direct Mail Mistake #2 is failing to make a compelling offer. People are hit over the head with so many TV, radio, billboard, Internet, newspaper, and magazine ads that they stop paying close attention after a while. Thousands of messages are constantly aimed at them. Your message has to stand out, piercing their shields of indifference. The offer must be so compelling it makes them want to do business with you quickly.

Direct Mail Mistake #3 is not using a deadline. Most

people don't bother with one. They make their special offer in such a general way that people think, "This *might* be something I want, but why don't I set this aside for a while? Maybe I'll get back to it later." You know how that story goes. If you're going to put it aside, chances are you're never going to order it. So use a deadline. Ten days is good. You don't have to put the exact date they have to respond by, because sometimes mail takes a while to get there—though if you're mailing to people in your area, it should be quite quick. Tell them to reply in 10 days from when they receive your fabulous offer, or it's off the table.

Direct Mail Mistake #4: Failure to offer proof. Show people that your claims are real. You can do so by carefully explaining the benefits, overcoming each objection one after the other, or by using testimonials.

Direct Mail Mistake #5 is failure to take advantage of direct mail's biggest benefit, measurable results. It's much easier to tell when you're getting results, and where they're coming from, than when you use the local Yellow Pages or PennySaver. Tell people where your business is, what you have to offer, and what they need to do to get it—and then keep an eye on who responds. This is one reason most advertising people hate direct mail: you can prove precisely what is and isn't working.

Direct Mail Mistake #6 is failure to follow-up. If you do a mailing and it works to any degree whatsoever, go back to those people later with other offers. Russ von Hoelscher likes to tell the story of the real estate agent who sent him mailings every month or so for years. She'd also send key chains, little calendars, and all sorts of things. Russ didn't intend to sell his home at that time, but appreciated the fact that she kept sending him things. So when he did decide to sell, he called her and had her handle it for a commission of several thousand dollars—all for $50 worth of trinkets on her end.

Direct Mail Mistake #7: Failure to cut to the chase. Make an irresistible offer; don't try to be cute or funny, or use the Madison Avenue style of advertising. I'm amazed by some of the ads on TV. Some are terrific and interesting, but when the ad is over, I can't understand or know what they're trying to sell. Be very direct with direct mail.

Direct Mail Mistake #8: Bad sales copy. Too many marketers use boring, dry copy that puts people to sleep. Use language that urges people to take action. Use words that hit people over the head, so they wake up and really pay attention to what you're saying. Learning to do this takes some time, so if you don't feel you can write compelling direct mail copy, then by all means hire someone who can—until you can do it yourself.

Direct Mail Mistake #9: Lack of diversification. Many people focus too heavily on one kind of marketing medium, limiting their potential. Overuse of traditional marketing media at the expense of direct mail is a common. When direct mail is used wisely, it can make you all kinds of money. You should never, ever neglect it.

This chapter covers both sides of the coin, because by revealing these nine major marketing mistakes, you also learn what you *should* be doing. There's a lot of bad direct mail out there; and once you have a feel for the right things to do, you can usually spot it pretty quickly. If nothing else, do the exact opposite of these nine mistakes, and you should prosper in your direct mail efforts.

When you sit down with someone who claims direct mail didn't work for them, you'll usually find that they made one or more of these nine mistakes, violating the core rules for successful direct mail. Sometimes direct mail won't work for some offers, and there are certain marketplaces where direct mail is less effective than it is with others. But more often than not it'll work effectively, when you follow the rules and avoid the classic mistakes. But be careful; you can have all eight of those other items right, but if you've got just one wrong, you can fail.

CHAPTER 3:
The Wisdom of P.T. Barnum

I'm a great admirer of P.T. Barnum, as you might have noted from my previous citation in Chapter 1. In this chapter, I'll discuss a secret that probably not one out of a thousand business owners truly understands.

Most people know P.T. Barnum from one of two things: either the circus that bears his name, or a quote incorrectly attributed to him: "There's a sucker born every minute." So one of the things he's most famous for is something he never said, and the other is something he did late in his life. But he was a sharp entrepreneur for his entire career, and this secret I'll share is a secret that made him so. It's one of the greatest secrets to discovering what it takes to succeed in direct mail, and in business in general.

The secret is to study the lives of people who have risen to the top. That's one of the reasons that I and many of my colleagues like reading business biographies. Studying successful people—including Barnum—is invaluable to your business. It's one of the reasons we like to coach people, and why we recommend that you have business mentors. The more you can study what other people are doing, the more successful you can be in your business—especially if you study people who have achieved success in the field you're trying to achieve success in.

P.T. Barnum himself was a brilliant marketer. In the

year 1877, which by most accounts was a typical year for him, the cost of advertising and publicity for his circus came to over $100,000—equivalent to $1.5 million in today's dollars. The lesson here is that you need to keep putting more and more of your money back into the marketing that provided your success in the first place. You need to discipline yourself to do this on a regular basis. One of the potential risks of newfound success is that you enjoy the spoils of that success a little too much—something you tend to see most dramatically in athletes.

An athlete might sign a big contract for tens of millions of dollars...and then you find out a few years later that they're flat broke. They didn't do anything productive with that money. You can sometimes fall to the same temptation in business; when you have success, you forget to repeat the thing that made you successful in the first place. Don't let that happen to you. Always plow some of your revenue back into what made you money the first time. Don't get overexcited by the money flowing in and go splurge. Direct mail is expensive; if you don't keep feeding the machine, you'll find yourself without the money you need to keep making more money.

The best strategy is to put a specific percentage of all of the money that comes in back into doing more mailings. Come up with a formula that works best for your model. For example, you might put 20% of gross revenue into an advertising fund. Then every week or every month—whatever your mailing schedule is—take that 20% and spend it on more direct mail. Do that, and your business will consistently grow.

Again, don't fall for the temptation of blowing all your

money as it comes in. It's a temptation we all face, especially the first time we experience success. The risk is that you want to pay off your car all at once, take a fancy vacation, or build that swimming pool out back with your newfound money. You *should* take a percentage of it and go have fun with it. You deserve it. You've built something successful and are entitled to enjoy it. But invest some of it for the lean times later, and keep a significant percentage aside for continuing and expanding your direct mail efforts. That way, you'll never find yourself without the money you need to continue fueling your business.

Let's look at a few examples of people who have failed to follow that advice. Russ von Hoelscher, of all people, once found himself yielding to the temptation. When he first started to make a lot of money as a young man, in one year he bought a Chrysler Newport, then a Thunderbird, then a Cadillac—one after the other. He also bought a house and a number of other things before he realized he was overdoing it.

Here's another example: I recently read about a man who played for the Houston Oilers football team and made about $70 million over an eight-year career. Last year, he was arrested in a 7-11 store in a suburb of Houston, robbing a clerk of $300 at gunpoint. That's a sad fall. For most people, $70 million would last a lifetime.

Similarly, I had a good friend who got started with the direct response business, hit it big right out of the gate, and soon had thousands of dollars a month pouring in every month. Suddenly, he had more money than he'd ever made in his life. What did he do? He went and rented a huge office, filled it up with office furniture and a phone system, bought all kinds of other stuff—and then didn't have any money to put back into the business. All of a sudden, he was broke. This is commonplace.

So spend your money, but make it serve you well so you can get more of it. Don't blow it! Too many of us just don't know how to handle money when we make a lot of it. If you need help, find a trustworthy financial planner to help you manage it.

If you want to learn how to make a lot of money in the first place, look at people like P.T. Barnum, people who have made careers of promoting big events. These people really have to know what they're doing to get people to flock in. You can also learn a great deal from evangelists. Recently, Russ was flipping through channels on the TV when he came across an old Billy Graham Crusade on a show called *Billy Graham Classics*. Graham was an excellent motivational speaker, and Russ tells me that he was struck by just how effective he was when speaking for the glory of Christ. He was at Madison Square Garden, and held 10,000-plus people in the palm of his hand. He was *such* a great messenger.

Pay attention to those people who know how to motivate, no matter their field, put their methods into action, and you will make lots of money. But again, be sure to set aside seed money for your next campaign before you start spending! It takes self discipline, but you *have* to do this. Put some of your money back into what made that money in the first place.

CHAPTER 4:
The Direct Mail Two-Step

In this chapter, I'm going to discuss the safest and most profitable way that you can make big money. Oh, you can make *more* money with some methods, but they're not as safe; in fact, there's usually some serious risk involved. After all, with big rewards come big risk...usually. But the method I teach here is surprisingly safe. Nothing is safer than two-step marketing.

This is another of the foundational principles behind direct mail. In Step #1, you're just trying to attract a highly qualified prospect using a well-designed low- or no-cost initial offer. Don't try to sell them too hard at first; just get your hooks into them, and educate them on whatever your product line or service happens to be.

Step #2 is to follow up aggressively. Once they've responded to the initial offer, the balance of power shifts to you. People hate to be sold anything, but they love to buy. What's the difference? When they buy, it's their decision—so make them feel like responding to you was their idea in the first place. Now you can bring out the big guns and tell your full sales story. Now you're in a position to show them exactly how you can give them the benefits they desire most. We've been using two-step marketing since the beginning, and using it with direct mail since 1989.

There are many ways you can use two-step marketing. Here's a quick example: When I recorded the audio this book is based on, I'd been working on a two-step direct mail campaign for the two previous days. I'd been thinking about it for a few weeks, rolling it around in my head, knowing I had to do this promotion. I'd had a meeting the previous Thursday where Chris Lakey and a few other people chimed in, giving me a bunch of ideas; and we had a nice little heated debate about where to go.

I do my most creative work in the early morning hours, so that Saturday I spent a few hours working on the campaign's direct mail letter, then I let it go. I went back on Sunday morning and spent another few hours with it; and I finished it that Monday. The package consists of a 4-page letter folded to fit in a #10 window envelope, with an 8.5 x 14 order form. The top half is the order form itself, the other half a voucher that shows them all they're getting for $99: a huge package with a retail value of $3,800. We use the miracle of technology to deliver that value in a digital format.

The outside of the envelope includes some teaser copy to get them to open it up. The voucher is personalized. All in all, it's a good-looking, simple direct mail piece that took me only nine hours to create...though more accurately I should say it took me nine hours and 20 years to create, given all I had to learn to do it right. It has the potential to make us hundreds of thousands or even millions of dollars. We test these packages to our best customers first. If they love it enough, we'll roll it out big time, and it *can* make us a fortune. We've done it many times in the past, and we'll do it again.

We're working on another direct mail campaign with a market size in the tens of millions, and that could generate

God only knows how many tens of millions of dollars—yet it might only take 30-40 hours' worth of creative work to put it together. Think about that. If the possibility of working for 30-40 hours and generating hundreds of thousands or millions of dollars doesn't excite you as an entrepreneur, nothing will!

You can use two-step direct mail for postcards, self-mailers, or packages like the ones I just described, but you *have* to test it on a small scale. Don't fuss over the cost; all that really matters is your return on investment, the ROI. You're one direct mail package away from making millions of dollars, depending on the size of your marketplace and how many prospects you reach with your direct mail. The greatest power of two-step marketing lies in the fact that you can introduce yourself to your prospects and *re*introduce yourself to your existing customers. You can make your lead generation offer free, and I've done it that way. But it works better if you'll get people to spend a little money on it—often as little as a buck or two—so they take you seriously.

If you're trying to sell something worth thousands of dollars, a small initial sale might be more like $100. Often you lose money on low-dollar offers, but the people who pay for them are now on your house list, and you can make them other offers. Getting them to response to a low-cost offer, as opposed to a *no*-cost offer, is the best way to get the prospect to come back and buy the more expensive back-end order.

Russ von Hoelscher once got fooled when he placed an ad in *Parade* magazine many years ago, when it went into 30 million newspapers around the country. Russ offered a free 120-page book. He ended up with 13,000 orders where he had to eat the cost; no one bought the follow-up. It was a disaster. That's how he learned to at least ask for a dollar or two for postage and handling. That cuts down the response enormously, because only the serious people respond—so your back end is more likely to succeed.

The best and safest way to make the most profit is always to attract a group of people who are interested in what you have to sell, then convincing them they should follow through and buy. That's the entire basis of two-step marketing. First cast your net, generating leads and building a prospect list. This is where you either rent a list or test the offer with your list of existing customers, people who already know and trust you.

If you're using a list of new people, you should definitely mail them a lead generation piece. This could be a postcard, or a brief sales letter reviewing your offer's biggest benefits. Hold back on the meat and potatoes, though; your only goal is to get them to raise their hand and request more information. Don't tell them too much at this point, or you'll risk them feeling like they already know everything, in which case there's no reason to buy. Be high on benefits and vague on specifics, making promises and emphasizing the reasons why they need to respond to find out more. Make them feel like you've left them hanging a little, so they need the fulfillment of receiving your package to be satisfied. Remind them that the only way to get that satisfaction is to request that information from you.

Here's where you separate the sheep from the goats. You can have a huge list of prospects, but the size doesn't matter if they aren't serious about your offer. We've actually told people things like, "Please include $20 just to prove you're serious," or "Please provide $5.95 to help with shipping and handling." From that point on, you can go to work converting them into paying customers. This is where you make your main offer to the people who have requested more information from you.

Let's say that your initial mailing went out to 1,000 people; you'll send the follow-up only to those who responded. That may consist of as few as 1% to as high as 5-10% of the total mailing. Suddenly, you've narrowed the list down to 10-100 people you can afford to spend more money following up with. It would be very expensive to mail several follow-up packages to all 1,000 of the prospects to try to get them to buy your product; but even if you had a 10% response, you have just 100 people who said, "Yes, please send me more information." It becomes much cheaper and more profitable to follow up three, five or ten times to those hundred people than it would be to send mail to the full 1,000 people—and you'll probably profit more in the end.

CHAPTER 5:
Right on Target

One of the reasons that direct mail is the ultimate form of marketing is that it's targeted marketing. You're using a rifle, not a shotgun. When you advertise in papers, magazines, or on TV or radio, you're "shotgunning" your offer out to all sorts of people, most of whom will have no interest in your service or products. Direct mail lets you zero in on exactly the type of people you want to reach.

That customization makes all the difference. You can spend your money to reach the people who are most likely to do business with you, not waste it on the general public. You learn what worked best and where they learned about your offer, unlike television, radio, magazine, or newspaper ads, so you save money. Your sales message can be confidential, personal, and one-on-one—and that's very powerful.

With direct mail, there are no limitations. You have total flexibility and control over the length and format of your sales message. Other forms of advertising make you conform to their rules; not direct mail. You have the power to make your sales message say what you want it to, and to ask for the offer in a direct way. When you mail 10,000 pieces of mail, it's like having 10,000 salespeople in an envelope. Don't get me wrong—I realize that if you had a sales force making calls, they'd probably have a better ratio of orders per people called than direct mail. In fact, it would be very unusual if they didn't.

But how many people can a salesperson reach in a day? Ten? Twenty? They're limited by how many businesses or consumers they can call or call on. With direct mail you can mail as many pieces as you like. They may not have the impact of the face-to-face salesperson, but they'll do a better job because you'll get more orders. Salesmanship is great, but few of us can afford to send a big sales team out to call on our prospects.

Direct mail is the ultimate marketing research tool, too. It's the ultimate way to reach new customers, and it's relatively cheap, because you can test-mail. You can make small mailings to start with; and then, when you see results, you can double, triple or quadruple the number of mailings you make.

I believe direct mail has proven itself to be a powerful communication tool, even in this age of electronic marketing. It's tailor-made for two-step marketing, and you can use it for any business. Some people think that if they have a store, they can't really use direct mail because all of their sales happen in the store—but that's not true, because it can bring people in the door who might never have come otherwise. It can make you a great deal of money—and you should get involved with it as soon as you can.

You know how a shotgun works; it sends out a spray of shot that hits everything within a certain distance. If you're using a shotgun approach to marketing, your message scatters in all directions. Mostly it hits the wrong targets. Radio ads, television ads, billboards, newspaper and magazine ads—all those are shotgun approaches. You message is wasted on most people. That's just the nature of a shotgun.

On the other hand, you've probably heard about sniper rifles, and how a really good sniper can hit a target hundreds or thousands of yards away. Rifles offer extreme accuracy. When you extend this analogy to your marketing, you're talking about precision and control, putting your sales message *exactly* where you want it for maximum impact. There's very little in the way of wasted resources. While you won't hit everyone, at least your mailing is reaching only people you already know are interested in the types of products and services you sell, whether you're a local reaching out to specific people in the community or a nationwide mail-order firm. Your list may consist of your own customers—people you've sold similar things to before—or a rented list of those who have bought similar things from other people.

The fact that a direct mail package is basically a sales rep in an envelope is particularly effective. You can present your entire sales presentation in an envelope thousands or millions of times, and never have to worry about your sales reps getting temperamental, tired, or depressed—and they never ask for a raise. When people open your envelope, you make them a big promise and a guarantee of what they're going to receive when they do business with you. If you use two-step marketing, you invite them to ask for more information. If you're a local business, you can invite them to come into your store for a sale or special event.

Direct mail *is* salesmanship. It's about taking the very best qualities you see in an entire sales presentation and reducing it to one package. It answers all the major objections a prospect buyer will have. It makes all of the benefits come to life and creates a great sense of urgency to get them to respond *now*. Your strategy can and should include lots of follow up. Earlier, I talked about a two-step campaign we're working on, where we follow up with a 44-page sales letter. During those 44 pages, we reveal everything. It gets people fired up, excited, and ready to go.

You can start small with direct mail, and grow it as your business expands. That's another aspect of total control; the scale is up to you. You can go as big as you can afford, or advance slowly. I love this aspect of control, as I believe any entrepreneur would. Control feels good. You're not giving your money to some magazine, paper, radio station, or TV station. You don't even have to give your money to a mailing house. You can do it all yourself if you want.

CHAPTER 6:
The Copywriting Formula
That Never Fails

The formula I'll discuss in this chapter will inevitably help you sell more things to more people. I recommend you find a way to incorporate it into all your marketing. Now, it may seem a little oversimplified; you'll no doubt learn more complicated, broader formulas later on. But this one will help you get started, and will help you think about how you should market your products and services. There are three basic steps, and I'll go into the details of each.

This is called the PAS formula; the letters stand for Problem, Agitate, and Solution. So: Let's start with a problem. Unless there's a problem, there's no need for a solution, is there? If I'm hungry, I need to eat. If I'm not hungry, I don't. If I'm a restaurateur, I want hungry customers. People won't come to my restaurant if they're full. I need to find out where the hungry people are, agitate their hunger, and provide the obvious solution of eating in my restaurant.

Start every marketing presentation and advertisement with the assumption that there's a problem that needs to be solved in your marketplace, and bring it to their attention. It's not enough to offer a solution if people don't recognize they have a problem. If you sell a cure for baldness, then your first mission is to convince people that baldness is a bad thing. That can be a problem if your market is comfortable with baldness. Similarly, if you're in the fitness business, the problem is that people are unhealthy, out of shape, or overweight...but you can't assume they see that as a problem. So make it one. Identify the issue you've got a solution for.

The second part is to agitate. Figuratively rub salt in the wounds by pointing out all the disadvantages they're experiencing due to their problem, and why it's important they care. Heighten their awareness of their dissatisfaction with their current state of affairs. If people are overweight, tell them how miserable they are. Their joints hurt, they get winded easily, their clothes don't fit as well as they once did, and other people may find them unattractive. This is where it gets a little sensitive, because if that's all you're doing, then you might be like that so-called "friend" who constantly draws attention to your flaws. But your purpose here is to introduce them to a solution. That's the only reason you want to bring up and hammer home how bad the situation is.

Then there's the solution, where you provide the cure for the pain you've just made real to them. By this point, they're eager to ease the pain—and your solution is the ideal way to do so. They're prepared to seek the relief you offer, whether it's a diet pill, a new hair-growth formula, or a gym membership, if they think it will cure what ails them.

Problem, agitate, solution. Again, it's not the end-all, be-all of sales copy, but it's a very simple, proven formula to guide you in your copywriting efforts, especially in the early days. Start by highlighting the problem, agitating it by making it real for them, and then offer them a solution that relieves their pain. This works for everyone: real estate agents, plumbers, electricians, barbers, booksellers, CPAs, or carpet installers. Businesses exist to offer solutions in particular aspects of the human experience, from clearing a clogged pipe to "the heartbreak of psoriasis"—a perfect example of PAS.

When I first got into direct mail and DRM, I decided the best way to make money was to help *other* people make more money, by offering them moneymaking opportunities. It works like a Rolex if you do it the right way—and one aspect of that is to apply PAS. I also learned something else: while people want to make money, they're even more interested in preserving the money they already have. So keep that in mind when you make these offers. If a person wants more, they'll always try to get more, but they'll also want to hang onto what they think is important. There's no question these are triple power plays; problem awareness, agitating the problem, and then offering a great solution.

Getting started with this copywriting technique is always the hardest part, so make a list of all the problems your product or service solves or potentially solves. Then start working on making all that real to them through agitation, before offering the solution in a way that overcomes their potential objections. Once you've done all that, combine all those bits of copy, rewrite and edit, and *boom*, you have a direct mail package. It's really that simple, though it does take time to develop.

Realize that people are *always* searching for solutions to their problems...whether they realize they have a particular problem or not. This is a formula you can use over and over. First you introduce the problem, then you make it real by personalizing it, and then you follow up with the solution. That's how you sell people. That's how you convince them that what you have is worth more than the money you're asking for it.

CHAPTER 7:
Maximum Profitability

In this chapter, I'll reveal how to make the most money possible from your efforts. All your biggest profits must come from this strategy, and that's simply to focus on reselling to your existing customers, by offering them additional products and services related to what you've already sold them. You can double or quadruple your profits this way. Most small business people are so busy chasing after new customers they're simply not spending enough of their time, energy, and money on reselling additional products and services to existing customers.

You need to realize just how insatiable your customers are. They're constantly hungry for more products or services. It's up to you to find those items, to work out joint-venture deals with others who can provide them, or to simply create new ones. It sounds like a lot of work, and it is—which is why so many people don't do it, even when they know they should.

If you're not constantly presenting and selling distinctly different offers to your existing customers, they'll start doing business with your competitors instead. They're going to give their money to *somebody*. They'd much rather give it to somebody they already know, like, and trust, rather than take a chance on someone new. You've already got a bond, and you must maintain it. Most small business people aren't doing this.

Direct mail is the world's most powerful method for reselling additional products and services to existing customers. In an earlier chapter, I pointed out that it gives you total control. That's one of its best qualities. You can develop new offers and send people postcards, self mailers, and direct mail packages again and again, with few if any rules to follow. Direct mail offers also provide a very good return on investment. You can make a profit even when only a small percentage of your customers rebuy. Let's say you have several thousand really good customers. You only need a few to re-buy on a regular basis for you to spend a dollar and make three, five, or ten dollars very quickly.

When you get right down to it, direct mail makes it easy and simple to keep in touch with your customers. It doesn't matter if you have a service business or have a store, you need to keep in touch with your existing customers even as you bring in new customers. You can't just wait for them to come through the door or pick up the phone and call you—you have to be proactive and contact *them*. If you want to make big profits, work with your existing customers all the time—even if this means finding something new to offer, or creating events out of thin air they can attend, so you can show them how much you value them.

Some companies are stuck in one mode. They offer one type of service or just a few related products, when they should get serious about acquiring or developing more products or services, or at least joint-venturing with someone who already has some.

Big sales can be made to existing customers because they know you, and hopefully trust and like you. We see evidence of that in direct mail marketing constantly. A good friend of ours once had a promotion that took in about a million dollars. When we asked him how many people he had to reach, the number staggered us: he replied that he needed to reach fewer than 500. Imagine making a million bucks using direct mail to reach fewer than 500 people! It really can happen, if what you're offering is right on the mark and they know they can trust you. In marketing to new customers. you're lucky if you get 2-3 orders by mailing fewer than 500 people. To make a million dollars, you'd probably have to mail flyers to 50,000 or 100,000 new customers.

This is an excellent illustration of how well you can do with even a small list of existing customers who trust you, people you've built a positive relationship with. I know that, like most people, you're anxious to bring new people to your door; so you're probably doing everything you can to build your new customer list. As you go about this process, though, don't forget the most important people, those who can make you rich: your existing customers. You'd better start treating them like the royalty they are, because they're literally your business's most important assets.

Too many companies, even big ones, just lose track of this reality. Some use new customer specials to attract prospects, at the expensive of their old customers. Take Direct TV: they do a super job of acquiring new customers, then do a terrible job of making you feel appreciated once you *are* a customer. They offer amazingly low prices to get you on board, but once you're a customer, you don't have access to any of those deals. A year or two after you sign up, your rates are super-high—and there's no way to get them low again except to cancel and then hope they make a good offer when you try to re-subscribe later.

You need a steady stream of new customers, but you also need to offer special deals to the people who have already done business with you. In most businesses, that's where the majority of profits come from: repeat business with existing customers. When you mail new offers, they respond the most because there's already a relationship there. The key to maximum profitability really *is* reselling to existing customers on a regular basis, using some kind of a formula for continuously putting offers in front of them.

Think of how Apple would do if they sold only the iPhone 1, or if they hadn't come out with other versions of the iPhone or iPod. They do so every year, just as they do with their computers, so they'll have a steady stream of new products and services to sell to their fans.

Continuously ask yourself what your customers want the most, then find ways to give them those things. Make them new offers for products and services related to what they already purchased from you. If you do this on a regular basis, your business will be flush with new orders. You'll be able to spend more time working on building relationships with customers and less time trying to figure out how to pay the bills. Remember: most people are insatiable. They'll always buy more. They're going to spend money whether they spend it with you or somebody else, so they might as well spend it with you. When you have an existing relationship in place, they're more likely to do so—and direct mail is the greatest way for you to make those sales.

CHAPTER 8:
The Golden Key to Success

How do you get everything you want? By giving other people what *they* want. The golden key to business success is to remember one simple fact: *never make a transaction about you.* Make it about your customers and what they want—not what they need. Their wants will make you much more money. You have to hit their hot buttons with your direct mail. Self-interest reigns supreme in your customer's mind. They're very passionate about what they want, far more so than what they need. The key elements of their wants are health, wealth, love, happiness, or derivatives of those. They also want to be recognized and appreciated. Do that, and they'll love you for it.

Realize also that they're all looking for a quick fix. When someone's in pain, any type of pain whatsoever, they want the fastest possible cure. They also want to keep what they already have. Recognize that, and look below the surface for what they're really after. If you fulfill those needs, you'll make a ton of money. Let me put this bluntly: to be an effective marketer, you have to understand how self-centered all human beings are. Get inside their selfishness and appeal to it with your direct mail, so you can make your offers so powerful and appealing they fulfill whatever need the prospect has.

The beauty of direct mail is that you can know in advance what the customers want. You can rent a list of people who have purchased certain types of health products, investments, or opportunities, or who enjoy specific hobbies or sports, and offer directly to them. Rather than making scattershot helter-skelter offers to everyone, you can tightly target your market. That's crucial. That's easiest with your own customers, because you know they like what you've sold before, and you already have that relationship in place. All you have to do is offer them things similar to what they bought before.

Always fulfill what the customer really wants. Not what they say they want or what you think they need—what they *really* want. Never forget that no matter what business you're in, no matter who your prospects are or what marketplace you serve, self-interest is the driving force behind purchasing behavior. This applies to every market. People will seek out products, services and companies that give them solutions to things they want, things they're interested in, and things that solve their problems.

A golfer will seek out products that help them look better on the golf course or help them lower their score. Those products won't interest non-golfers. If they're gardeners, they'll look for shortcuts and solutions that make gardening more efficient or effective, whereas someone uninterested in gardening won't respond to ads or offers for such things. Your success in your chosen marketplace is dependent on your ability to promote your products and services in ways that play to your marketplace's self-interest.

Needs are important, but we rarely have a "want" for things like toilet paper, toothpaste, or deodorant. They're just needs. We buy them because we have no choice; and that's a negative thing. You don't choose to buy, you're driven to buy;

so often you get the cheapest things that work. Maybe you just need to smell good so people won't avoid you, or you want to avoid huge dentist bills. Leave those markets to the people who can operate on razor-thin margins. Small businesses need to stay within the framework of items that people really, really want: fun things, bling, or the incredibly useful. The more they want it, and the more you can provide solutions to them based on those wants, the more successful you will be.

Earlier, I mentioned insatiability. Find yourself a market of insatiable people and leverage that factor. In many marketplaces, the more people buy, the more it inflames their desire to want to buy even more. Most business owners and entreprencurs fail to realize that, so they're not offering their customers *nearly* enough related products and services. If you will, you'll have a leg up on the competition—and there's simply no better way to make more offers more efficiently than with direct mail.

Having been in this business for a quarter of a century, I talk about it all the time with people I meet. Every time I've ever told someone we get mailing lists that our competitors put on the market, and then mail our offers to those lists, they act like they can't believe it. They say, "Why in the *world* would your competition put their customer lists on the market?" Well, that's how it works in DRM. Once you've rented those names, you can throw your bait out there in the form of a great direct mail sales letter, and have a much better chance of reeling in profits because you know you're making the offer to people who have bought similar things before.

Eventually, you'll want to put your mailing list on the

market too, because it serves everyone. It's good for you and the marketplace, in that its value increases the more you put it out on the market. Those people on the list will buy from your competitors anyway, whether you're putting your list up for rent or not—remember, they're insatiable. You might as well make money renting your list, inflaming their desire to want more—which is the whole point here. We're talking about matters of the heart. These are emotional issues. Never forget that.

CHAPTER 9:
A Checklist for Writing Direct Mail Copy

In this chapter, I'll introduce another superbly useful formula: an 11-point checklist for writing direct mail copy that sells. Put these tips to work, and watch your sales and profits soar. All 11 of these points are important ways of ensuring that your direct mail sales copy does an effective job of getting a rise out of your target market. Good sales copy will always deliver the results you're looking for, assuming you have the right offer for the right marketplace and the timing is right—whether you're trying to get someone to request information from you, to convert a prospect into a customer, or to do more business with an existing customer.

Point #1: Does the copy sound simple and easy? As you read through it, take out anything that makes it sound difficult. Keep the language that makes your solution sound effortless; anything else will hurt sales. But be careful; don't misrepresent the process. Stay entirely within the framework of honesty; just steer clear from making it sound hard. This may be as simple as chucking all the $5 words and replacing them with everyday words. The easier it is to understand and do, the more likely people will see themselves doing it—and the more likely they'll be to buy.

Point #2: Is the offer a pile-on? Does your copy pile on the benefits higher and deeper? If not, change it. Write an improved list of the benefits you can offer your prospects. List off all the things the prospect will get when they respond to your offer—just like in the infomercial world where they say, "But wait! There's more! You're going to get all this, *plus* the kitchen sink!" If the kitchen sink isn't there, you're not offering enough value for their money.

Point #3: Have you done all you can to jazz it up? Here's where you need to make sure your copy isn't boring. It must be appealing to the reader, exciting to them; they're already interested in your product type, assuming you're reaching for the right marketplace, so make them even *more* interested. How is your offer different than everyone else's? Make your copy entertaining, but not necessarily comedic.

Point #4: Write out a list of objectives. Ask yourself, "Did I answer them all?" If not, then do so. Ask yourself, "What's my goal? What do I want the end result of this copy to be? What are my specific objectives?" As you're finishing your copy, go through your list and ask yourself if you've answered them all. If not, go back and add them in.

Point #5: Have you done everything possible to inject your personality into every page? Most direct mail is personality driven, written from your own first-person perspective. Write one-to-one, as you'd write to a friend. Write to a specific hypothetic person; you can even give them a name in your head. Use your personality as a lever to convince them they should be doing business with you. Delete the generic language.

Point #6: Build legal defensibility into the copy. The marketplace you're in somewhat dictates what you need to do here. In all DRM, it's important to carefully follow all the rules, regulations, and laws that govern how you can sell your product. This may change occasionally, so keep an eye on the laws; don't get caught flat-footed. Whatever field you're in, there will be legal ramifications to your copy. In our litigious society, people can sue you for anything, especially if you've said something incorrect.

There are many ways to make your copy defendable. For example, we always talk about the *potential* to receive the various results we sell; we never guarantee or promise it will happen. If something requires a little work and the purchaser won't do it, then they won't get results; but if we said they would no matter what, they might sue. Careful wording is critical. And remember: there are a lot of regulations that govern the direct response industry. Look out for those legal pitfalls that could trip you up.

Point #7: Is there a strong reason for the offer? If not, find one, especially if you're offering them a lot for a little. Otherwise they might become so suspicious they won't buy. If you offer thousands of dollars worth of value for $99, tell them why you're doing it and how it's possible. Be honest, and you'll build credibility.

Point #8: Why do they need to respond right now, without delay? If you let them wait to respond, then they probably won't. People who delay action usually don't take action, so tell them why they must respond now and make it easy for them to do so.

Point #9: Is there a strong cutoff date with a good

reason behind it? Specify a hard date they must respond by. Many people won't believe an offer is time-limited otherwise. Too many marketers have flippantly used generic cutoff statements like "You must respond in ten days to this limited offer!", and then not actually stopped their sales on that date—so the generic cutoff has lost its effectiveness in most marketplaces. Plus, open-ended offers give people excuses not to respond right away.

Point #10: Does the mailing look and feel different than everything else they're getting? An offer in a plain envelope won't get the attention it deserves. Try things like sending a letter by priority mail, UPS, or FedEx instead of in a regular envelope, or put commercial messages all over your envelope to tease them about what's inside. Or go the other way and make it look like a letter from grandma, so they're more likely to open it. Some people try to make it look like a bill. You can include grabbers or "freemiums," as we call them, to make the package lumpy—which makes them want to see what's inside.

Point #11: Are you offering payment options? This isn't necessary for some offers, but if you sell expensive packages, make it easier for them to say yes by offering them the ability to split their payment into multiple payments. We've allowed as many as 12 for some of our more expensive offers. That makes it easy for them to get started faster; they don't have to save their money or wait to take action. We're all used to making payments on houses, cars, credit card bills, etc. Your buyers will like having the option, so your sales will increase.

Here's a bonus 12th point to consider: add testimonials,

especially if you operate a service business. People want to see that other people are happy with your work. And another thing: before you start, decide very carefully which mailing list you'll use. Lists of your existing and best customers work at least 3-5 times better than any other list that you can use. If you're building new business, it's important to work with a highly regarded list broker.

And finally: get on as many mailing lists as you can! When you start getting tons of direct mail from a lot of different companies, you'll see how these previous points are being used in the real world. They'll become so familiar that it'll be easier for you to start doing these things without being prompted.

It may take some hard work and study to implement this checklist, but it's worthwhile because it's extremely profitable.

CHAPTER 10:
The World's Biggest Marketing Mistake

Earlier, I quoted one of my heroes, P.T. Barnum, as having once said about marketing, "Most people are trying to catch a whale by using a minnow as bait." The man was a brilliant marketer, and this is a wonderful metaphor for the field, because it fits so well. Even now, people are trying to build fortunes by being cheapskates. It doesn't work that way, folks. You don't get big results anywhere, in anything, without investing massive effort and big money.

Direct mail is the most expensive form of marketing, outside of hiring a commissioned sales representative to go out and beat the bushes for you. Ah, but marketing is all about salesmanship, and as I've mentioned before, that's what direct mail lets you do best. You need to spend money and effort on it to make it work. You wouldn't just send a salesperson out and say, "After five minutes, I want you to shut up." That would be insane. No, you tell them, "I want you to do whatever you have to do to get that sale. I want you to answer all their objections. I want you to pinpoint all of the biggest benefits we provide. I want you to tell the complete sales story."

That's what a good direct mail package does. Yet so many people just want to mail postcards or little self-mailers—tri-folded cheap flyers—and then they wonder why it doesn't work. It doesn't work because it never stood a snowball's chance in hell of working. They don't know what the hell they're doing.

There's no avoiding it: *direct mail is expensive if you do it right.* Some of our sales letters are up to 50 pages long, but they do a complete job of selling. We use a 44-page sales letter to promote one of our programs, and those 44 pages tell everything there is to tell about it. But because it's expensive, we use two-step marketing to promote it. We send a small direct-mail piece first, consisting of a four-page sales letter, a 8 1/2 x 14 order form, and a #9 return envelope that all goes into a #10 envelope. It weighs under an ounce, which makes it very cheap.

This particular mailing offers them two options. Option #1: they can send for our 44-page report. But we're still trying to catch the whale, no question about it. That 44-page letter tries to sell a $99 initial offer; then we step them up to a $1,000 offer. The next sale after that is a $3,500 offer, and the next is just under $5,000. Option #2 is for them to send in for the $99 offer directly; many do, which offsets some of the cost of the direct mail package, therefore making it even less expensive. This example represents a very inexpensive direct-mail package, but it leads to a series of follow-up pieces. We aren't just throwing a four-page letter out there and expecting to get rich. That's what so many others are doing with direct mail. They have unrealistic expectations. They think they can spend a little money and a fortune will roll in—and they can't!

Long-form letters are very expensive, but can be very profitable when used intelligently. Remember, the average customer needs all that info, because we have no personal contact with them. They can't easily ask questions, so we have to answer all their questions in advance. We have to stress all the benefits we're offering, and make those benefits easy for them to understand. Also, you have to realize that people are going to skip over a lot of what you have to say; you have to repeat yourself several times in those pages, so they still get the information.

Most small service businesses and retail stores won't require that much volume in their sales letters. They can send a 2-6 page letter to explain a new product or invite folks to the store. If they're smart, they'll tell their customers they have a limited supply, and to come in quickly. If it's a service business, they'll discuss what great benefits they're offering. They can do this in just a few pages, offering a free quote. So there's a difference between those of us who have no contact with our prospects, and those who have a store or service business. They can use fewer pages and still get the job done.

But they still have to make it simple and easy to understand, the copy must be exciting, it must be full of benefits, and they have to overcome all objections. They should also set a time limit for the response. Spend more time on sales copy when you lack direct contact with your customers or prospects; that's when the long-form letter comes into its own. Otherwise, it may not be necessary. The message is valid in either instance. If you're fishing for whales, don't use minnows for bait. If you're using the wrong method to attract them, they won't to find you. They don't have the time. They'll go with the first lure that attracts their attention.

These people are already spending money on other

things in your market and others. They're actively engaging other businesses, but for some reason they aren't finding yours. It could be that your product or service is wrong, but if that's not the case, then it's probably the things you're doing (or not doing) to attract those customers that's holding you back. Change your approach, and see if that helps. Sometimes making minor adjustments can pay huge dividends.

Now, in some cases P.T. Barnum was wrong. You *can* use a minnow as bait and catch a whale. My earlier example is one such case; yet, that's just step one of a multi-step process that continues to sell more and more items. Good marketing is a process; there's a series of steps you have to take in order to catch those whales. Each step leads to another, and direct mail is the perfect format for taking each of those steps.

CHAPTER 11:
Fulfill Their Secret Desires

In a previous chapter, I talked about the desires people have that they're aware of. They want more love, happiness, money, recognition; they want, they want, they want. Those are the things they *know* they want; but now let's get into secret wants. This topic is both a lot more engaging and more difficult than learning what customers know they want. The fact is, many people don't really grasp their true desires—and in fact may have camouflaged them with other things they think they should want instead.

So it's very important to understand that millions of people have secret desires that aren't being fulfilled. They're quietly searching for someone to fill their desires, even though, in many cases, they're not quite sure what those desires are. Now, before this gets too metaphysical and difficult to understand, let me present an example that should make things a lot clearer for you.

Donald, a sharp operator Russ von Hoelscher knows in San Diego, runs an insurance agency. Among other products, he sells life insurance and annuities. He told Russ that people come to him and want life insurance because they want their families to be taken care of if something bad happens to them. So for many years, he's sold products that have filled those needs. But being a sharp man, he eventually realized that people wanted something more than just to provide for their families. They never talked about it, though maybe they had a hint of it in the backs of their minds.

You see, they wanted to get some benefit from the money they were paying out month after month, year after year. So Don found new products that would not only pay off to the family if the person died, but also give people some of their money back after a certain period of time. He told me that's when the sales went right through the roof.

People really did want to take care of their families—no question about that. But he found and exploited that secret desire, which was to get some of that money back while they were alive. I hope that gives you some idea of what I'm talking about.

Whenever you talk to your customers, look for their secret desires—especially if you have a one-on-one relationship with them. Look for not just what they *tell* you they want, but what they *really* want and may not even realize consciously. If you do that, you can make a ton of money. But how do you figure out what those things are? Well, you know what they consciously want, so what other ways can you appeal to them? That varies according to the market. If you can get to the point where you understand them even more than they understand themselves, then you've gone to the center of their intellect and desires. If you can get into their subconscious minds, the results can be highly profitable. This is the heart of the psychological aspect of selling.

Let's assume you've already matched your potential audience with your offer. When someone receives your direct mail offer, they have to make a decision about whether it's interesting enough to read your sales letter, then respond by visiting your website, coming into your store, or dropping the order form in the mail. Many of the results you receive depend on these secret desires—the things people don't talk about and may not even understand.

Now, these desires aren't secret in the sense that they're something your prospects don't want to tell you, it's just that they don't consciously recognize those desires. They don't always even understand why they buy what they buy. So it's up to you to get inside their head, and to learn the things about them that they don't realize. The better you can do that, the more successful you'll be.

Chris Lakey sold cars for a year when he was about 20 years old, and one of the things they teach you is to figure out what a prospect is thinking about when it comes to buying a car. They might tell you, "I want a sports car. I'm looking for a minivan. I want a truck," but they don't necessarily tell you why. You have to do a little fishing, asking questions that get them to talk more so you can try to discern what the underlying reason for the purchase is, then sell to that point.

If someone is looking for a safe vehicle because they have a newborn child, you need to figure that out so you can talk up the vehicle's safety features. If a 20-year-old college boy comes in with no family to care for, safety features aren't that important; he wants speed, power, and looks. You do some digging, find out who the prospect is, and determine their underlying reasons for buying—not just what they say they want. Then you steer them to vehicle that gives them that the things they want the most. That increases your chances of making a sale.

This works in any marketplace, though often it's more "one-to-group" than one-to-one. If you know your marketplace intimately, you'll soon start to discern more of the underlying reasons or factors behind their buying behaviors. Then you can craft your sales message in such a way as to deliver those results based on their secret desires as well as their professed ones. Even though they may not be able to express those desires, they remain tremendously important, lurking in their subconscious and influencing their buying decisions on a level they don't really appreciate.

As difficult as it may be, you *must* learn to recognize those issues and how to sell to them. Spend time getting to know your marketplace and the consumers in it so you recognize those secret desires, helping them on even on a deeper level than they realize they need help on. I realize this point may not be easy to grasp, but once you *do* get it, you'll realize just how critical it is to create offers people really want to respond to.

Good DRM is all about is psychology and mathematics—and by and large, direct mail math is easy math. All you use are addition, multiplication, and division. That's as easy as it gets. Self-interest rules the world here, because when it comes to spending money, people are the most selfish creatures on the planet—even when they're otherwise unselfish people. They're very cautious, often for good reason, and all they care about is "What's in it for me?" Your direct mail has to appeal to that self interest—to the point where it positively reeks of it.

Often, people are buying in a vacuum, ruled by unconscious emotion. The only way you'll determine what appeals to them is to carefully observe them and test things over the course of years. It takes an intimate knowledge of your marketplace to determine exactly what their secret desires are. Always look for those desires. It's up to you to figure them out, so think deeply about the types of products and services you sell, and what's behind it all. What emotional desires are they seeking fulfillment on?

Sometimes you have to spend years thinking about and studying these issues to come up with your best answers. I'm not pointing this out in an attempt to discourage you, because you can certainly earn while you learn. It's just the reality of the situation. Few people burst on the scene with their products perfectly matched to the market's needs. Just keep at it, and your best ideas will get better and better—and you'll end up making more and more money.

CHAPTER 12:
Turn 30-60 Minutes a Day into Huge Success

If you'll just spend 30-60 minutes a day tightly focused on your direct mail efforts, you can generate huge success. I know this for a fact, because it works for me—and if it can work for an everyday joe like me, it can work for you, too.

So many business owners spend so much time working *in* their businesses that they never actually work *on* them. You might get to the end of the day and know you were busy all day long, but when you look back, you can't pinpoint anything productive. There are a lot of things that go into making your business run, like working on payroll, paying taxes, trying to balance your books, operating your cash register, ordering supplies and products, fixing equipment, and dealing with crises. If you spend all your time and energy on these things, you may wonder where all that time went and why you're accomplishing little more than a holding action.

As I've said before, you make money by selling more to existing customers and bringing in new customers, so find a little time in the day when you focus on nothing but that—especially in terms of building your business through direct mail. It adds up, and the results will be seen in increased activity, increased sales, and an increase in customers coming into your store—all of which will result in increased revenue for your business. So take some time, sit down, and start documenting some ideas on how to improve your business and develop better offers.

If you're most comfortable in the paper and ink world, you might start with a yellow legal pad and pen. If you prefer the digital world, type into MS Word or a similar word progressing program. Make sure you have plenty of your favorite beverage on hand. If you focus early in morning, as I do, that might be coffee; if you're a night person, diet soda or herbal tea might work better. No matter when you spend your time on your business, just spend that time. All it takes is 30-60 minutes, focused specifically on writing sales copy or on coming up with copy ideas for ads, sales letters, fliers, brochures or anything else you're doing via direct response. Concentrate and develop specific sales copy and techniques you can use for your business.

Remember: it's important at this point in the game not to feel that you have to spend that productive time producing a whole sales letter or order form. This could be time spent jotting down headlines, sales ideas, or offers you want to make. Whatever the case, it's focused on putting copy on paper that you can use in one way or another. If you'll do that for an hour a day, that's 365 hours of nothing but thinking and dreaming creatively per year. If you just spent 30 minutes a day, it's half of that—but it's still almost 200 hours over the course of a year.

Maybe you started out not doing anything like this; maybe sales copy is a new concept for you, or you've only dabbled in it a little. But if you commit an hour a day to writing sales copy, you'll learn vastly more about marketing, you'll learn more about selling by mail, and you'll become a better copywriter all around, assuming you're using the right principles and strategies. You'll end up with more sales copy going out to your marketplace, because you'll be turning some of these ideas and thoughts into offers. That will increase your activity, potentially increasing your sales and profits. Ultimately, that focus on sales copy and ideas will be productive for you.

This is critical, especially in a small business where the owner wears all the hats.   This limits your focus on things that actually result in increased business. So make time for this strategy. All of those other things will still be there, but you'll find yourself energized and excited about your new ideas and daily productivity. Looking at it right now, it might seem like a daunting challenge; but when you look back six months or a year from now, you'll see the fruits of that labor. This won't take anything away from what you're already doing; quite the contrary. It adds something that will have a measurable impact on your bottom line. No question about it.

We all know that focus is the important thing—and most of us know we don't focus like we should. But it's necessary to spend time looking at the potential and problems in our business, and then to strive for the right solutions. It all comes from that type of focus. If I've said it once, I've said it 1,000 times: most people work *in* their businesses, not *on* their businesses. The most successful entrepreneurs and business people are those who spend time focusing on improvement. Just being *in* the business becomes a morass of phone calls, problems to be solved, meetings, distractions, and all the other things that are really just parts of the machinery of business and day-to-day consumption. When you get outside the business, in your mind's eye at least, you can focus on what's important.

I advise everyone to consider doing this. I get up about 5 AM every morning and focus on business. I especially like thinking about direct mail math. Recently, we tested a postcard for $500 per thousand. These postcards give away an absolutely free book—we're opening the funnel as wide as we can, getting as many prospective buyers as we can to call a toll-free number and listen to a one- or two-minute message. We're making it easy for people to say yes, and very hard for them to say no.

If we mail 1,000 postcards for $500 and get a 5% response, that means 95 out of every 100 people throw the card in the trash can—but five want the free book. That's 50 leads per thousand, or $10 a lead. See how easy it is? Of course, there are some fulfillment costs, and I'm excluding those. In this case, the free book is a digital download from a website, so there's very little hard cost there. If I pay $10 a lead, what do I have to do to get that money back right away? How many initial sales do I have to make? I'll spend hour after hour just running it all through in my head.

This gives me confidence. Thank God direct mail math is simple! You just have to know what it costs, what percentage of response you require to get a certain number of leads, and then the amount you need to make on an initial sale to be able to spend a certain amount of money. So I would encourage you to dream, scheme, plan, plot, and think about all the different ways you can make money with direct mail during a specific slot in your schedule.

It all starts in your head; money is born as ideas. It's the quality and quantity of thinking you do as you're working on it, rather than *in* it, that truly matters.

CHAPTER 13:
The Easiest Way to Make Big Money

Want to make big money? All it takes is two steps: a basic two-step marketing strategy. If you do it right, it works like a money machine, cranking out large amounts of cash anytime you need it. And it's so simple I could explain it to one of my little grandkids—if I could get them to pay attention.

Step #1: Segment out the best customers on your customer list. **Step #2:** Make them an irresistible offer, something so good they just can't say no. If you do that, you can potentially put huge sums of money in your bank account. It's so simple you can't afford *not* to try it. That's common sense...and yet most business owners don't see it that way. They don't realize that their best customers are insatiable and that they're going to keep buying if given the chance. So they aren't doing enough to develop additional related products and services they can resell to those people repeatedly.

First, identify and separate out your best customers, based on specific criteria. We label our best customer groups A, B, C and D. Group A represents people who spend a lot of money with us. Groups B and C represent the people who spend within certain ranges. By the time we get down to Group D, we're including anyone who spends $100.

We go to Group A—our very best customers—first,

doing everything possible to make them a great offer. And that's what we sell: offers, not necessarily products and services—though an offer does include a product or service as its foundation. It may also include a free bonus gift, special prices, reasons to respond right away, special guarantees, and other incentives. You package things up and pile it on, to the point where they just can't say no.

During the first few years Eileen and I were in business, our sales flatlined right after Thanksgiving. They picked up again in January, one of our biggest months. But right after Thanksgiving, people have the holidays on their mind; that's all they're thinking about... and it just destroys sales. Now, Eileen loves Christmas time. It's her favorite holiday. But for the first eight years of our business, I was so grumpy then that I'm lucky she didn't divorce me. I made Christmas hell for her.

Then I decided that I was going to use this two-step marketing principle of going to our best customers and making them an irresistible offer, even though it was Christmas and everybody had the holiday on their minds. I put together one hell of an offer, and the money came rolling in. I've done the same every year since. Sometimes December is our very best sales month now. About one out of every three years, we get it just right; we create that irresistible offer and get the ultimate December. We try to do it every year, and we use this simple concept I've described here. We go to our very best customers, make them an offer they can't refuse, and the money just comes pouring in.

Of course, we include that magical element where we say, "This offer expires on midnight December 31. When the clock strikes midnight, the sale is over." Since people are thinking about the New Year, it works. It's a simple idea, like so many of the others I discuss in this book—but don't let its simplicity fool you. This concept can be worth millions to you, assuming you have enough customers and create the right offer.

Meanwhile, I especially urge you not to forgo your regular customers in favor of chasing new customers. Too many business people are so hungry for new business they neglect the business they already have. I've seen it over and over, and it's almost like criminal neglect, because people are tying their own hands, limiting their own profits. You will ALWAYS make more money with your present customers than from prospects who have never bought a thing from you.

In addition to being in direct response marketing for over 35 years, Russ von Hoelscher has owned motion picture theaters and small chains of bookstores. At one point, one of his bookstores was located next to an antiques store. He got to know the woman who ran the store, which was fabulous and large. She had some of the most unique items he'd ever seen, so he'd often go in there and browse. Eventually they got to talking about business, and he said to her, "You must have a good customer list. How long have you been in business?"

It turned out she had been in business for five years and didn't have much contact with her customers. Russ just about fell over. Here she was, selling items that cost several hundreds or thousands of dollars—including a few Chinese Ming Dynasty items, among other rare and semi-rare antiques—and she had no customer list!

Russ did her the favor of telling her how important a list was, and how to go about building one. He suggested she offer an incentive by putting a jar on the counter for people to drop business cards in, and to have some blank paper people could fill out with their names, addresses, phone numbers, and e-mails if they lacked business cards. Once a month she could draw a card out of the jar and give the winner $100 worth of store credit. She liked that idea.

It just goes to show that many small businesses don't even know who their customers are. They might recognize some by face, because they come in once a week or once a month, and may actually get to know them...but they have no idea who the majority of their customers are. They couldn't send them a direct mail piece if they wanted to, because they don't know where they live. Usually, they don't even know their names. It's critically important to capture the names and addresses of your customers before you even start a direct mail campaign. If you haven't been doing this, start doing it immediately. Your customers are your most important asset.

Frankly, I find it difficult to believe that some businesses continue to exist, given how poorly they communicate with their customers. There have been times where I've given businesses permission to communicate with me and never heard from them again. As a marketer, I have to wonder why they bothered collecting my contact information if they weren't going to use it.

Give your customers a reason why they should want you to have their contact information. Make a special offer, or have them sign up for an email newsletter. Let them know you want to stay in touch, so you can make them special offers by mail, and then collect contact information. Once you've done that, the easiest way to make more money is to focus on those customers. It defies all common sense to ignore existing customers, fighting constantly to attract new customers, not even bothering to try to make existing customers feel special, giving them a reason to continue to come back and do business with them again. But businesses do it all the time.

Existing customers are where all the money is. It's usually easier to get them to do business with you, and it's cheaper to make the sale, because you've already developed a relationship with them. They already trust you, which makes it easier for them to say yes to a new offer. You spend less time and energy following up. Why would you ever throw away that easily-sold audience in favor of someone you have to chase to get any attention at all from?

Start with that as a premise, and you'll improve your business. You'll make more money than when you were focusing on new customers. Don't forget the people who have already done business with you. Make a list of them. Reach out to them. Make them feel special, with a compelling offer that tempts them to rebuy. You might hold a customer appreciation sale on a certain night only, where you stay open late and they need a ticket to get in. Get creative and have fun with it, but do make them a compelling offer to continue doing business with you. That's the easiest way to make money quickly.

And remember—it's not about the size of your mailing list, but how you use it. I have a good friend in Dallas who had a mailing list of fewer than 300 of his best customers, which he developed when he was speaking at marketing seminars. He generated many hundreds of thousands of dollars by sending those people multiple direct mail offers for years. It just goes to show that you can make a lot of money with a small, carefully cultivated group of really, really good customers—as long as you strive to make them what you honestly believe are irresistible offers that they can't refuse.

CHAPTER 14:
Ogilvy's Laws

In this chapter, I'll discuss one of the most famous advertising and direct response marketing men ever: David Ogilvy. The man was a genius, legendary in the field. In fact, he turned that field upside down many times. Today, I'll reveal 12 of his best secrets, which you can use to dominate your marketplace. He revealed these in Paris at a big advertising conference, and absolutely shocked the entire audience. It's powerful stuff and, for many of those there, it was a hard truth to face—but it *was* the truth.

While Ogilvy was and remains highly respected, he shocked a lot of people when he said these things in that convention back in the 1950s—so much so that I'm sure the room got very silent and people eventually walked out. He took the stage and said flatly, "There is a huge chasm between you generalists and we direct marketers. We directs belong to a different world, and your gods are not our gods." He went on to say, "You generalists pride yourself on being creative, whatever that awful word means. You cultivate the mystique of creativity. Some of you are pretentious posers. You are the glamour boys and girls of the advertising community. You regard advertising as an art form, and expect your clients to finance expressions of your genius."

I suspect the mainstream advertisers and the Madison Avenue types didn't care to hear this, not to mention what came next. His third point was, "We direct marketers do not regard ourselves as artists or regard advertising as an art form. Our clients don't give a damn whether we win awards or prizes. They pay us to sell products, nothing else."

Number Four: "You must be the most seductive salesman in the world if you can persuade hardheaded businesspeople to pay for your kind of advertising, because I know what this is about. When sales go up, you claim credit for it. When sales go down, you blame the product." I'll bet a pin could have dropped in the room and it would have sounded like thunder.

Number Five: "We in direct response know exactly, to the penny, how many products we sell with each of our advertisements."

Number Six: "You generalists use short copy, we direct marketers use long copy. Experience has taught us that short copy doesn't sell very well."

Number Seven, "In our headlines, we promise the consumer a benefit. You generalists don't think that to do that is creative."

Number Eight: "You have never had to live with the discipline of knowing the results of your advertising."

Number Nine was, "We pack our advertising and letters with information about the product. We have found out that you *have* to do this if you want to sell anything." Truer words were never spoken.

Number Ten: "Act eccentric while you're young. That

way when you're old, people don't think of you as going gaga. You don't think I'm gaga, do you?"

Number Eleven: "Unless your advertising contains a big idea, it will pass like a ship in the night."

And Number Twelve: "Remove advertising, disable a person or firm from proclaiming its wares and its merits, and the whole of society and the economy is transformed. The enemies of advertising and direct response are the enemies of freedom."

What a powerful speech he gave! What a powerful way to tell them that, "We in direct response marketing have to measure *everything* we do, and we are found to be successful or unsuccessful in any project that we get involved in based on the end results." He was telling the Madison Avenue advertising types, "You don't do this. You just throw things on the screen and make up a nice jingle for TV, radio, magazines or newspapers; and if it works well, you want all the credit. If it doesn't work, you tell the client their product was no good."

I can just imagine him delivering this presentation to the Madison Avenue advertising executives of his day, people who were probably aghast that he was talking this way to them. Even today, these advertisers are smug in their certainty that their way is the *only* way, and they're high and mighty about the fancy ads they produce. They like to win awards for having the best-looking ads...but they don't necessarily care about helping their clients make the most money possible. I can just imagine the horror as they listened to a man they considered one of their own present these ideas to them. I wish I could have been there, watching this speech take place, just to see how people reacted as Ogilvy challenged the status quo—especially his contention that they'd never had to live with the discipline of knowing the results of their advertising.

One of the greatest things about direct mail is that you can know without a doubt if it worked or not. It's not good for those ad agencies to find that out for sure, because many times they discover that what they're doing *isn't* working. But you, of course, want to know if your advertising is producing results. With direct mail you can know exactly how much it costs to produce a mailing. You can analyze your results and know how much profit you brought in. You can counter that with your fulfillment expenses, and know to the dollar whether that mailing made a profit or not. It's accountable in that respect, and that's very valuable, because you must know what's working and what isn't.

Another thing Ogilvy pointed out that makes special sense to me was his Number 9 item: "We pack our advertising and letters with information about the product. We have found out that you *have* to do this if you want to sell anything." Unlike other advertising methods, direct mail is specific about the offer or product. Other advertising is light and fluffy, made to look good or fun—but doesn't do any hard selling. We pack our offers with information about what our products will do for people, and the end results they'll achieve when they use our product or service. What he's laid out here is a blueprint for success in direct mail. *This* is what we do in the direct mail world, and *this* is why we are successful. He draws a stark contrast between what they do in the creative world of Madison Avenue and what practical marketers do.

Ogilvy was a rebel, and I respect the spirit behind his

ideas. As I've pointed out before, direct mail marketing is salesmanship in an envelope. A direct mail letter offers all the best qualities of the greatest salesperson you can imagine. You hone and perfect it, get everything just as nice as you can, and then put it all into an envelope—sometimes a small one, if you're using two-step marketing.

The first step is to get people to accept a low or no-cost offer and qualify themselves, then follow up with a bigger envelope with more stuff in it—but it's still all direct mail to me. It does everything a good salesman does, and gets the right person interested. It makes them want to know more. It tells the full sales story. It answers and overcomes all the objections the prospect has; and last but not least, it closes the sale. This is every single thing you would expect a good salesperson to do—only cheaper.

CHAPTER 15:
Make More Profit
in Three Easy Steps

In this chapter, I'll discuss a simple three-step direct mail marketing system that gets more people to give you more money, more often, for higher profits. Isn't that what you really want? The main thing I want to emphasize here is that a good marketing system focuses on the prospect more than the product, in all ways. Think about what you sell, and think about the marketplace you sell to, and remember: when it comes to direct mail marketing, who you sell to is *much* more important than what you sell.

You see, no matter what you sell, the marketplace you serve will remain more or less constant through time. Your business might survive for decades, and the products and services you offer throughout that time will come and go; but the people you sell to will generally be the same (assuming you don't change marketplaces altogether).

Now, some changes do occur. People will come in and out of the marketplace and some clients will stop being customers—but the marketplace *as a whole* will stay mostly the same. So you have to know that marketplace better than you know yourself in order to sell to it. If you start with the premise that you need to do a better job of understanding who your customers are and who the marketplace is, then from that position, you'll be able to identify the kinds of things that marketplace wants.

I've discussed in other chapters the process of identifying the benefits people are looking for. Usually, they seek out offers that fill their wants or provide solutions to problems they're experiencing. If you're in the diet industry, people who are overweight will seek your solution to help them become fit and healthy. If you're an electrician, you solve people's electrical problems. If you're a mechanic, you fix people's cars. People come to you because they're in pain or have a problem they need solved.

If you always start with the marketplace, then the products or services you offer can adapt and adjust as you serve them; whereas if you start with your product or service and your marketplace shifts, you're stuck with worrying about your product specifically. You may miss the market shift because you're so focused on your product, and may be unable to keep up because of that focus. So: step one in successful marketing is attracting the right kind of people and repelling all the others. You do that by means of the offers you make, based on your extensive knowledge of your marketplace.

The second step is building people's trust. Today, it's not easy to trust people, especially in business. Many businesses have let people down in all kinds of ways; and in fact some of those problems go far beyond individual businesses, straight to the industry at large. You have entire industries full of problems, and then governments get involved to try and fix the problems, sometimes creating a whole new set of problems.

As a small business owner, you have to break through

that distrust by building relationships with people. What better way to do that than with direct mail, where you can communicate with them one-on-one? It's as if you wrote a letter specifically to them; it can introduce you to them and establish that relationship. As they continue to do business with you, the relationship can grow stronger. In the beginning, when you send your letter to a prospect who doesn't know you from Adam, it's the only thing that *can* build any kind of relationship or trust factor. You have to use words to paint a story that introduces them to you, your company, your business, and those benefits they can achieve when they decide to become your customer. Direct mail is perfect for that, because it's a one-on-one communication. It's not a billboard they see as they drive down the highway. It's not an ad they see screaming at them from the TV.

No, it comes quietly in the mail and, when done right, delivers a hard-hitting benefit, promise, or guarantee that makes them sit up and take notice. You can then build from that point and ultimately gain their trust, which is how you survive in business. You don't do business, especially repeat business, with people you don't trust.

The third step in this formula is proving to them that you alone can provide them with the things they want the most. Again, we're talking about the marketplace here, not just the product or service you sell. You want to prove you can deliver the goods, make good on your promises. You have to convince them you have something they can't get anywhere else. That's where your unique selling position or USP comes in.

Give them a strong reason why they should trust and do

business with you. If it's too easy for them to get what you have from somebody else, they won't have a good reason to decide to do business with you. The more you can deliver the idea that they can't get what they want somewhere else, the more likely they'll be to choose to do business with you.

If you'll do these three things—attract the right people while repelling the others, build their trust through the offer, and then prove to them that they really need to do business with you and you alone—you can get more people to give you more money, more often and for more profits. You have to do these things right, or you'll chip away at your profits. I've used this strategy effectively for years, and so have many of my colleagues. Remember: lifelong customers are always more important than a particular profit or offer. If you make them happy, they'll eagerly await what you have to offer next. That should be your goal: acquiring lifelong customers by attracting the right kind of people who come back again and again.

Now, this doesn't work equally well for all businesses; a realtor won't be selling houses to the same people every week or every month, but they can still build a relationship for sales years down the road. With smaller products and services replaced on a continual basis, of course we want our customers to do business with us as often as possible. This is true no matter what marketplace you're in: real estate, moneymaking, health, investments, home products, home improvement, or professional practices. You want a continuous flow of customers, both new and repeat business. If you're smart, you take care of your good customers and keep them coming back again and again.

One way to build trust and get new business is to use two-step marketing. This works like a Rolex. You offer a low- or no-cost product or service, not making a profit from this first step. The idea is to bring in a flood of new business, and then follow up with a great offer that makes you money later. Always keep in mind that your best customers deserve your best services and products.

The third step I mentioned was giving people what they want—not what you think they want or need. This is key to all business success. When you're looked upon as the primary source for a specific kind of product or services people want in your area, you're going to make money hand over fist. When people trust you, when they know you have what they want, whenever it comes to mind they think, "Oh, I've got to go see Bob." You're the source. That's the ultimate power to make money, especially when you're the #1 source in your community. If you want a realtor, you have to see Jack. If you're getting a massage, you have to see Betty. If you want a plumber, you have to see Hal. Whatever your business is, you want to be the source. Again, it's all a matter of building trust with your market.

Don't be afraid to tell your story. In fact, you *must* tell your story. Now, you might ask, "What *is* my story?" It can be lots of things, but ultimately it's how you connect with your prospects and customers. What is it you can dramatize that will connect you to them in an emotional way? Only you can decide what that is. Your story can be of how your company came to be, the story of how you came to discover and develop the products and services you sell, or the things you have in common with the people you're trying to do business with.

Find the most compelling way to tell your story, and tell it often. You'll get sick and tired of telling it, I promise you, but they won't get tired of listening. People want to do business with other people just like them. People love emotional stories, and direct mail is the perfect way to do that, because you have room. You can write quite a bit about your story and include pictures that do a full job of illustrating and describing the kinds of things I'm talking about here. The old logo for direct mail, before they changed it, used to be a close-up of two people shaking hands. It's that personal connection that you make with people that matters.

Remember, this is all about salesmanship. The best salespeople build a rapport with the prospective buyer before they go in for the close. You have to do that with your direct mail, too.

CHAPTER 16:
The 100% Safe Way
to Take Bigger Risks

The greater the risk, the greater the reward. We've all heard that saying... but we also know that by taking bigger risks, we can lose everything. What you need is a safe way to take those risks, and that's what I'll reveal in this chapter. Just remember this: it's not about what something costs you, it's only about what it *makes* you.

If there's one marketing sin that people commit over and over again, it's that they try to spend a little money in an attempt to make a lot of it. The only thing you should focus on is ROI: return on investment. It's dollars spent versus dollars made. Nothing else matters. Here, you try to generate the largest number of the most highly qualified prospects you can find, knowing that will profit you more in the long run.

Once you've got a qualified prospect, you have three main strategies: you can upsell them, down-sell them, or cross-sell them. Upselling is just making them a bigger offer, or giving them more of what they bought from you the first time. If you plan it right, you can purposely try to sell them a smaller package that makes it easier for them to make an initial buying decision, and then you go for the upsell. Upselling has probably been done on you many times, so now you have to get on the other side of the cash register and start doing it to your prospects and customers.

Or you can down-sell. You can go for a higher-priced package first, using direct mail; and then you can sell a lower-priced package. As you can imagine, we don't do much of that. Cross-selling is more common. This is just a fancy term for selling people additional related products or services similar to what you already sold them. All the repeat business you do with people—that's cross-selling.

The secret to upselling, down-selling and cross-selling is to use direct mail and then follow up like a madman. Be relentless in your follow-up. Don't give up on them too soon. Many years ago, we lost, quite possibly, millions of dollars because we spent a small fortune to create an infomercial and tested it in 17 cities. It was an initial lead generation offer, where they could watch our 30-minute show and then send away for more information on our $3,000 product/service combination absolutely free.

A lot of people from those 17 test cities sent away for that free information—but we just couldn't convert enough of those leads to sales. We gave up on them far too soon. We failed. Had we known then what we know now, we would have practiced what I just told you. We would have followed up like crazy. We would have rained direct mail on their heads and would have only worried about ROI. We would've then tried to down-sell and cross-sell to all the unconverted leads, offering additional products or services that were semi-related to what we were trying to sell them for $3,000. There's so much you can do—but most people are just giving up on their prospects too soon.

As I write this, we have a really hot lead generation

piece that delivered close to 1,000 leads today. Before we even know what the conversion rate is, we're trying to sell them a $1,000 initial package; but then, we have lots of different options. We have natural upsells, down-sells to the unconverted leads, and plenty of cross-sells. And before we even know how this promotion is working—because we know where the leads came from, and we've been working with the type of people all of these leads represent for a long time—we're fairly confident we can sell them lots of different things.

ROI is always the bottom line. Once you total up all the costs of a mailing or program, do you have a profit left over? There might be dozens of things you'll have to take into account, but when you know your exact expenses and the response you get from your mailings, you can easily determine the ROI—whether you sent out 5,000 or 100,000 mailings. As David Ogilvy pointed out in his Paris speech, in direct response advertising, we know our costs, and we also know what came in.

Mailing lists are crucial here. We know the best lists are our own customers, and I'll talk about that in more detail soon; but first I want to talk about the costs of mailing lists. Good list companies charge from $100-150 per thousand for good response lists. Those are lists of people who have spent money for certain types of products or services. If you have a similar service or product, that's one of the best lists you can get.

Now, there are other list companies that claim to have response lists that charge as little as $20-30 per thousand. A lot of people are fooled by that; they think, "Why should I pay $100 or more per thousand when I can get a list for $20 or

$30?" This goes back to what I said earlier about being willing to spend more money to do things right so you can reach the right people. The cheap lists don't work. They're old, tired lists filled with nixies—addresses that are no longer accurate, so your mail can't be delivered. So, yes, you spend $100 or more to get 1,000 names, or thousands of dollars to get tens of thousands of names; because to give $20, $25 or $30 to these rascals with cheap response lists is a foolish mistake.

I know this is true because I've made that mistake. Ultimately, these lists cost you a small fortune because you get very few orders and a high percentage of your mail comes back. Also, beware the "print and mail dealers." Most of them are thieves. They offer super-low prices to print and mail your advertising for you, but when you add it up, you can see there's no way they can do it for the prices they charge. They'd be in the poorhouse. So always be willing to spend more to do things the right way, and to reach the right customers. That's how you make money in this business.

That's one of the reasons M.O.R.E., Inc. has a strong preference for direct mail, and why I've urged you to know your marketplace. It limits the risk, so you can take bigger risks without losing more money. Ultimately, because you're able to track your results, you can know within a few cents or a few dollars exactly how much money you've made or lost with every promotion that you do. If you want to run two or three different promotions at once, you can track all of them—just be careful about it.

The problem with traditional advertising is that while you may know exactly where you're spending your money, you have no clue where your customers are coming from. The advertising is too general and isn't keyed so you can tell what generated each response as it occurred. You can't tell where the 10 customers who just walked through the front door came from. Which ad did they see? Did they watch the ad on TV, or find it in the newspaper, or in the Yellow Pages? Was it a radio ad that worked, or that postcard you mailed?

When that happens—as most ad companies want it to—there's no way to figure out the ROI. Oh, in the abstract you may be able to calculate some of the loose numbers, but there's no way to specifically account for each dollar of advertising. Did it come from upselling, down-selling, or cross-selling? You have to constantly look at those options and know at least that much, because not everybody buys. It will never ever happen. Some of each new group of prospects coming into your business aren't going to respond positively to your offer; so you need to know that, and need to use some kind of alternate method to try to get them to respond. That may be making them another offer related to what they were interested in already, or maybe down-selling them something cheaper. Maybe they need that option to get started.

As I've pointed out, customers either buy or they can be up-sold, down-sold, or cross-sold from that point forward. Again: it's all about calculated risks, knowing your marketplace, and then working to turn as many people in your marketplace into customers and then repeat customers from there. There are specific strategies for doing all three types of selling, but it comes down to doing as much repeat business as possible with all the leads and customers that you have. You should be relentless about it—and there's no better method for that than direct mail marketing.

It's stealth marketing too, because when you're using direct mail properly, your competitors don't know what you're doing at all. You can generate massive amounts of sales and you can do it all behind their backs.

CHAPTER 17:
The Essence of Direct Mail

As I've stated before, your mailing list is more important than anything else in direct marketing. You can write the best direct mail letter in the world, but if it doesn't go to the right people, you're going to lose a lot of money. The list is absolutely crucial to your success. So let's take a look at the best mailing lists you can use, starting with the very best: your existing best customers.

These are the people you can mail to and count on getting a great response. If you mail a new offer to your best customers and get a poor response, you don't want to mail that to anybody else without making some significant changes—because it isn't going to work. The people who have done business with you for the longest period of time and have spent the most money will tell you quickly whether a new service or product is what they want. These things determine how seriously people consider what you're selling.

Your best customers always want new and interesting things from you. They trust you and feel strongly about your company—but if it doesn't work with them, then it's not going to work with anybody else. Even if it *does* work with them, you have to note the degree to which it worked, because there's going to be a decline in response as you go to on to other lists. The response must be strong enough to bother.

The next best list is occasional customers and past

customers who haven't done much business with you recently. At the very least, they've bought from you once. These occasional people are still a prime list to mail to, though nowhere near as good as your best customers. The next best list would be referrals from happy customers. These would be people who are probably going to pay attention to your direct mail: people who have shown some interest, but have never become customers. They may have contacted you and asked for information about your services or your products, even if they never bought anything. While nowhere near as good as the previous lists, these are often people you can make a nice profit with.

Those are the best ways to deal with people who have had contact with your company. Beyond that, the next best list to use would be a response list—people who have bought a product or service similar to yours, though not from you. A good response list from a reputable mailing house can make you a lot of money. In some ways, that response list could be as good as or better than the occasional or past customer, or the people who just inquired with you—although, for the most part, anyone who has contacted you will usually give you a better response. I'd make a response list #5 on our list, going down.

At the very bottom would be a compiled list—a list of people who not only haven't spent money with you, but for whom you have no information concerning how much they've spent with others. They've obviously done some business with other companies, but otherwise there's little information on them. Realtors, insurance salesman, senior citizens in a given area, homeowners—these are all compiled lists. There are thousands of them. Now, don't misunderstand me here, because a good compiled list will work very well for some things.

For example, the owner of a shop that sold surfboards in Pacific Beach, whom Russ von Hoelscher got to know many years ago, simply mailed to people who lived on or near the ocean in San Diego. He got all kinds of business from mailing to Ocean Beach, Pacific Beach and La Jolla. He didn't design surfboards, but had a friend who did, so he had both commercial boards and these very special boards from a real artist. He made a ton of money just by mailing to people who lived on or near the ocean. The list that worked like gangbusters for him was just a compiled list.

Recently, Russ also spoke with a gentleman who was selling a newsletter on making money with blue-chip stocks. He tried the same approach as the surfboard shop, but began with a list of people who lived in rich areas like Palm Beach, Beverly Hills, Rancho Santa Fe in La Jolla in San Diego, and some very exclusive areas in Boston and New York City. When Russ asked him, "How did this work for you?" he told Russ that he broke even with this approach.

Now, if you break even with a newsletter, you did pretty well—because when it's time for them to re-subscribe, *that's* when you start making money. So he was willing to lose money on the front end in an attempt to acquire customers, since he makes all his money on renewals. That's a hard thing to do, but it works with wealthy customers.

Most projects and programs that are mailed to compiled lists don't work very well. Though to use another of Russ's examples, he did work with a guy who wrote a book and later turned it into a cassette tape program up in Seattle, Washington, based on how to make money by becoming a real estate agent. Some topics included how agents can make the most money and things you're not told in school. They were able to get the names of new real estate agents who had passed their tests in the states of Washington, Oregon, and California. Every month there were tens of thousands of names coming in from those three states, with California leading the way.

Russ and his friend sold the program originally for $99.95, before raising the price a little bit later. This gentleman became a multi-millionaire—just by selling information to new real estate agents, showing them a few selling tips and then helping them invest their income in real estate for themselves. That worked well.

The bottom line is that compiled lists are the bottom of the barrel for most of us in DRM—but for certain types of services and products, they work very well.

What I've discussed here is the blueprint for how we run our entire business model with direct mail. It all starts with our preferred list of best customers. Whenever we have a new promotion, the first thing we do is let all our very best customers know about it. These are people who have done business with us recently and those who have spent at least $100 with us.

If they get excited about it and we get a good response, we make that offer available to our next best list: people who have spent less than $100 dollars with us, or who might have not bought anything in the last year. We have a relationship with them, but don't consider them preferred customers. If those people respond well, we'll move on to our next best list and make an offer available to the marketplace in general, people we have no relationships with. If it works there, we'll use it for new customer acquisition.

The key is to always test, especially if you're working with a new list. It would be a mistake to take a brand new offer straight to people you have no relationship with, though you may have to try that if you don't already have a customer list. If you're brand new, you have to start somewhere; in which case, you may want to start by joint venturing with someone. Find someone who has a list and can endorse your offer for a split of the proceeds. You can also do this if you're already established and want to tap a list you have no relationship with. It's much better than just renting a list in your marketplace, a list with which you have no connection to at all. A third-party endorsement sometimes can make all the difference in the world.

And let me re-emphasize: Most small business people are NOT doing enough to resell to their current customers. This is one of the ways we can easily help most small businesses double their profits very quickly, just by taking this reasonable, logical first step. That's what Russ taught us when we started working with him to add direct mail to our business. The $2,500 a weekend we paid him—which would be worth about $10,000 dollars now—was worth every penny. Following his advice, we generated millions of dollars very quickly, just from offering new products and services to existing customers, items that were related to what they'd bought before. It was so simple! He wrote up the sales copy, we had it typed and sent out, and we raked in the money.

Spend more time with your existing customers. That is the most powerful thing you can do. That mailing list is everything. You've got to keep testing and trying different things with them, and direct mail is the ultimate way to do that. None of the other strategies I've revealed in this book are worth anything if you're mailing your offers to the wrong list—no matter how perfect everything else is.

CHAPTER 18:
Five Steps to Creating Powerful Promotions

The simple formula I'll reveal in this chapter can be your #1 secret strategy for getting the very best prospects in your marketplace to do business with you. Some of these steps will sound familiar, because I've mentioned them elsewhere in this book, but they all bear re-emphasis.

Step #1: The marketplace is more important than the product or service. Remember that one? Yes, what you sell is important; it plays a role, obviously, because it's what people are buying. But if you don't start out by understanding your marketplace first, then no amount of good products or services will cure that. You have to have a good understanding of who you're selling to, and that's much more important than the exact products and services that you sell.

Step #2: Write your sales material first, based on the biggest wants, hopes and fears of your marketplace. This assumes you're offering something like information marketing; if you sale a widget and it already exists, obviously that's not a possibility. But if you sell paper-and-ink, audio programs, or Internet-based information products of any kind, this is a very important step for you. Write your sales material *first*, after you've become an expert on that marketplace. This lets you create an offer from the very beginning that delivers on what your marketplace wants the very most.

Step #3 is to make the biggest promises you can while still being believable. Believability is important. It doesn't matter whether or not you can do something; if people don't believe you can, you might as well leave it out. You must be able to verify a claim, or you'll hurt sales by including it. Just because something *can* be done, that doesn't mean that you necessarily want to tell them that you'll do it—unless you can make them see themselves receiving that benefit.

Step #4: Include specific information to make the offer more believable. Generalities are too vague to make people believe; specifics, as opposed to generalities, will help you close the sales. Use facts, figures, testimonials, and similar strategies to verify that what you're saying is true. This helps build trust with your marketplace and helps them feel confident doing business with you.

Step #5: Use your sales letter as a template to create the ultimate product or service. Again, I'm talking about information products here. Once you've done all you can to create that perfect sales letter for your marketplace, you have the blueprint for creating your product. Suppose you've written a sales letter that promises your prospects 10 things if they do business with you. Those 10 things become the formula and outline for creating your product. Whatever you're writing—a book, a course, or audio program—use the sales letter as a guide to deliver all those things to your customer. When they receive your product later, they'll have everything you promised them.

That's the basic five-step formula. It works especially

well if you're creating information products, but can be adapted to anything. Just start out with a marketplace in mind, figure out what that marketplace wants the very most, then offer to give that to them. If you can deliver, you'll never want for money.

The most important factor here is trust. They have to trust you at all levels, or they won't give you their business. Once you say something that they feel is a lie, they're going to stop reading your mail. They have to like and trust you, and trust is the more important of the two. Verify your claims. Don't just say they can make $10,000 a month; show them how. Show them how, if they make $10,000 a month, $50,000 is a possibility. Having customers who are already making that kind of money is an even stronger argument. As long as people trust you, they will give you their money—especially if you stand behind your claims.

Local businesses can offer a guarantee. There's a really well-known car dealer in the San Diego area who says, "Buy this used car from us, take it home, test drive it, kick the tires, do everything you want with it—and if you don't like it in seven days, bring it back and you owe nothing." That's a promise most used car salesman would *never* want to make, because you're telling people they can have a free car for a week. I suspect they qualify their customers very well, making sure they're not dealing with any nutballs. Apparently this offer has made them a lot of money.

If you're a dentist or chiropractor, you can guarantee your work. If somehow a tooth breaks off or the partial plate isn't right, you'll do it over anyway; so why not guarantee it? That makes it sound better. Likewise with *any* product or service you're selling. If you can guarantee it, do so, because it builds trust. When you're dealing with a plumber who guarantees his work, you feel very good about the plumber—and this works for all kinds of other services and for many products.

The most important step, I think, is #2: Create your sales material first. I realize that some people may think this is totally insane, yet nothing could be smarter, because customers are really buying the benefits, not the product or service. They're after the perceived results based on the promises you make to them. This works better for some products and services, but let me tell you this: you can pretty much do this with any service. There are so many intangible aspects to a service, and all kinds of shortcuts, strategies and insights you can use to jumpstart the process. People buy benefits. Creating sales material first may sound crazy, but it will produce a tremendous number of sales.

Also, before moving on I wanted to return to the concept that prospect knowledge is more important than product knowledge. Now, in some ways knowing too much is a bad thing; you can get hung up on the details. Just know what people want. Get in their heads and find that out, because again, people buy benefits, not features. A benefit is the emotional end result they can get if they buy your product or service. You can load it up with lots of benefits, make lots of promises, and then get busy scrambling like crazy, trying to figure out how you can fulfill on all of those promises. Think outside the box!

CHAPTER 19:
The Things That Sell the Best

In many cases, the products and services that will sell the best and make you the most money are surprising and somewhat ridiculous—things your competitors would never dare do. Consider the car lot I mentioned earlier that allows you to drive your car free for a week before committing. I'll bet when people do bring that car back, they don't get out of there without some serious high-pressure from the salespeople.

You have to do outrageous things just to get people's attention these days. We live in a marketplace that's truly oversaturated in many ways. Now, I'm not trying to be negative here; the positive part of all of that oversaturation is the fact that it's being done by the blind leading the blind. Most marketing is homogenized and boring. Nothing really stands out—and that is the key to what I'm trying to describe here. You've got to do things that shock people, things that wake them up. You have to do things that generate tremendous excitement: things that sound really good, with big, bold promises people notice. People remember it when it's crazy, over the top, even a little scary. I think things that scare you a little are actually good.

When you're using direct mail, there's one point you cannot forget. Let's say you have a list of a thousand good, qualified prospects. You can have a wild, crazy, obnoxious, over-the-top offer and only send it out to 50 of those people. It could be something where if it doesn't work and you mailed it to the entire list of a thousand, you would lose a lot of money. But if you just mail it to 50, yes, you might lose some money, but you're only going to lose a little. That's one of the beautiful things about direct mail. You can spend a lot of money creating big, elaborate direct mail packages that do a complete job of selling, then only mail to a small portion of the list. If it works, you roll it out to the bigger list.

We call it lumpy mail, because you often put all sorts of trinkets inside the package to make it bulky. These things cost you money, but that's just another example of doing things that are ridiculous and surprising. They're surprising because they're different. We're living in a market and age now where everybody is afraid of offending other people. They're afraid to stick their necks out. You can't make that mistake. You *have* to be a little crazy to get noticed.

Direct-mail is the perfect way to test. Let me give you a couple ideas of how we've done it here at M.O.R.E., Inc. In one case, we were testing a bunch of different front end offers for new customer acquisition. We scheduled 10 different test mailings, where all I was doing was changing the headline on page one of a 12-page sales letter that sold a low-cost offer. I ran out of ideas on the ninth one, so I used what I honestly believed, at the time, was the most obnoxious, dumbest idea that I could think of for the 10th. It was dumb in the sense that it violated all the rules of direct-mail.

There are standard protocols, you see, things that have been proven to work. One of those is that a headline should be fairly short, simple, and to the point. On this 10th test piece, I created a headline that took up almost the entire first page of the letter, using lots of words in a large font. I never expected it to work, but it outperformed the other nine by a long shot. It became our control, which meant we kept using it, testing new pieces to see if we could do better. We mailed millions of those letters...all as a result of an accidental discovery. Sometimes I think we try too hard. We want to get it perfect, and I fall prey to that all the time. In this case, I just threw it out there—and it worked.

I think you should test as much as you can using direct mail. Look for things that are newsworthy, and outrageous offers like the San Diego car dealer's. Look for things that would just scare the hell out of all of your competitors to try—and that even scare you a little. As long as you're testing small, you don't have to worry about losing a lot of money. If it works well—and it very well might, because it does go over the top and grab people's attention—you can make a fortune. I've seen it in other markets, too. Some of the most outrageous offers are some of the most successful. They're shocking, they're different, and they capture the imagination.

Another thing that I've found works exceptionally well is to make people feel special. Offer them something exclusive, something most people will never have, and they'll get excited about it. On the show *60 minutes*, I once saw a piece about a restaurant in New York City that charges the most outrageous prices in the world—but they have no prices on their menu. They even have a sign in the restaurant that says, "If you need to know the prices of the food we serve, you shouldn't be here." You might think it would insult people who go in there and aren't told what they're going to be charged. But they're *always* busy. It's crazy what some people can get away with!

Another thing that really gets people's attention is to tell them the unvarnished truth about your offer. Tell them it's great, it's powerful, it's something they should have—but it's not 100% perfect. Russ von Hoelscher once sold phones for a dealer who had gotten them for a very good deal. (They weren't cell phones, because this was many years ago.) Among the things Russ wrote in the advertising was, "These phones are as good as any you'll ever find on the market from AT&T or anyone else. There's only one thing wrong with these phones: Every one of them is black."

Sales went right through the roof, because people didn't *care* if they all were black when they could save so much money. So tell the truth about the product, and also tell the truth about yourself. Show them you're a flawed human being. Tell them about some mistakes you've made in the past, how you've overcome those mistakes, and how you've found something special you want to share. That's a powerful thing.

People love stories, and a story often told in the moneymaking business is, "I was broke. I was dumb. I didn't know what to do. I found this miracle way to get rich. I'm rich now, and I'm going help you get rich." Hell, that's *my* story. It's true. I think that was a powerful thing at first, but there are so many clowns using that story now that I can't help but believe that it's nowhere near effective as it used to be.

Just tell the truth about yourself and your products, while putting them in the best possible light despite that truth. You can even tell people things about yourself that you might not want them to know. The late Gary Halbert was famous for this. He wrote some ads for a client who was apparently involved in some illegal activities, and he was actually sent to jail for a year and a half. The average person would keep their mouth shut about this. But in his sales letters and newsletters, Gary talked freely about it. He even wrote a manual about his experiences in a federal penitentiary: what he learned there, what was good about being there, and also what was terrible.

People really appreciated Gary. Russ knew him a little; he was apparently kind of a hardass and hard to really get to know, and in person he kept people at a distance. But in his writing he came across as an open person with no secrets who would tell you anything. Thousands of people gravitated to him, to either subscribe to his newsletter or to hire him as a copywriter—and he was a very good one.

Shock people. The bestsellers often wake people up from their mundane existence. Most of us are living routine lives in which we do the same things every day, over and over. There's very little to distinguish one day from the next. As a marketer, you have to get people to open their eyes and pay attention to you. People are so busy with their own affairs that they sort of float through life, going through their routines and sometimes missing good offers they might love. That's why you need to create offers that really do surprise people and get them to pay attention to you.

One caveat: These must be legitimate offers selling products and services you can deliver on. Don't shock them with lies; even if your statements are outrageous, prove they're true. When you do that, you get people to pay attention—and more importantly, you get the right *kind* of people to pay attention, while repelling the rest (at least for this offer). You have to do things that stir emotion in them, get them charged up, get them alert, awake, and ready to respond to your offer.

If you're using direct mail, you can do that without worrying about losing your shirt. That's the good news, the one strength that no other form of selling has except for using live salespeople. But a real salesperson costs you a lot more money. Direct mail is more fun and lets you do it more economically, in a way that completely and totally separates you from everybody else.

EPILOGUE:

Thanks for reading *Direct Mail Mastery*. I hope that you'll read it again, and come to know these ideas intimately. Live with these ideas. Mark up the chapters, highlighting the sections that make the most sense to you. Add little sticky tabs that let you go straight to those sections, so you can reread them when you need to brush-up on these methods. At the very beginning of this book, I told you that direct mail marketing and this book itself could change your life and business. It may have sounded like hype when I said it then, but if you've read the whole book, you know that it's the truth. You now know how to wield direct mail as the profitable weapon it is in the war against the competition. And make no mistake: it *is* a war, one you need to win.

Just by using the strategies I've gone over in this book, you'll have a tremendous advantage over your competition. Know also that there are a lot of great marketing secrets that I didn't go into in any detail in this particular book. You can buy our other books and audio programs, and use those secrets in conjunction with everything I've discussed here.

If you need someone to critique your copyrighting, be sure to contact Russ von Hoelscher and take advantage of that special offer I made on his behalf at the very beginning of this book. Russ is a direct mail master; without him I would have never learned the secrets of direct mail, and I would never have been able to teach them to others. If you need his help, don't hesitate to contact him. If you need additional information from us, or if you'd like some of *our* help and support, then contact us. I've tried to do everything possible to share the best direct mail secrets with you in this slim volume, which contains the greatest hits, tips and strategies that I personally know of for making tremendous amounts of money with direct mail. I've used these methods to make millions and millions of dollars. This should be just the beginning for you, though, and we're more than happy to help you move to the next stages of DRM.

Let me repeat: I urge you to reread this book over and over again. You'll notice things the third and fourth times through that you didn't the first few times, and other things you did notice will sink in better. Think about all this very deeply—and then start applying these things to your business.

You'll soon see the results as your sales and profits rise.

CPSIA information can be obtained
at www.ICGtesting.com
Printed in the USA
LVOW10s2048280518
578715LV00001B/121/P

long. Small rainbows rose to a hatch of Blue-winged Olives in the downstream, small, unexpected pool, but though here away from the cliff the afternoon sun still angled down from just over the hillside and into the area under the current tongue, in what was now the upper pool, I saw no fish, browns or otherwise.

The current was now so soft that I could see individual rocks, could probably get my stonefly nymphs to the bottom without any additional weight, but I saw no reason to, and after a last look I turned back downstream towards the trail out, my car, and a cup of something warm. This was not the pool I had thought to fish; it had departed for the season and would return around the first of August, just as the fish to fill it did.

Made in the USA
Middletown, DE
13 December 2015